Sal visiting his 10 comrades who tragically were killed in air gunner training exercise march 29th 1943 at Morpeth cemetery 50 years after the accident.

To My Wonderful Family,
With Fondest Love,
Dad

ACKNOWLEDGMENTS

Thanks to Rika Pais, for her excellent translation and hard work in producing this war diary of Sal that has been sleeping unknown for over 80 years.

To Fay Muller, my mother who without her incredible encouragement and support through their time together this book would have no story.

To Scott Muller my son, who found the war diary and has been instrumental in building the history of his grandfather and the family.

Geoffrey Muller for whom without his relentless passion to see this project through, we might never have seen it brought to completion.

FOREWORD

Courage and fortitude, standing on the shoulders of migrants, the giants who have shaped the world as we see it today. Papa Sal's story is not one of unique scarcity but, at times, a life experience that hundreds of thousands of us across the country would have recognised within our own origins, our own history. If, of course, we're lucky enough to know. This sensibility is just how things were for Sal's generation.

Fortunately for us as a family, and not everyone is lucky enough to receive such a gift, my grandfather, Papa Sal, had the foresight to keep a record of his life experiences and wrote a wonderful memoir before his early passing at the age of seventy-two.

Papa Sal's book 'Aim for the Top' has been in our family for decades. He gave such an incredible insight into the life he led and his incredible experiences. For us who followed him, there is much strength in knowing about our past, our heritage. It's what informs our identity and has forged many of the values within my brothers and me, learnt from our parents, which have been passed through the generations now into my children, continuing the legacy.

I read his book in my teens for the first time and now again most recently, and it was from this most recent reading which I had the imagination to try and encapsulate Sal's story into a poem. The struggle being, how might it be possible to reduce such a well-lived and extraordinary life such as his into a comparatively minuscule piece? I struggled with the idea that even to try could be disrespectful, almost frowned upon, a heresy. Who was I to condense a man's life down into a string of pithy lines, but as the idea grew and finally putting pen to paper, done well, the poem would be a truly heartfelt standalone piece of poetry, my gift for the family.

Two copies of 'Aim for the Top' were all that were ever printed for the purpose of the family to pass around and share. Over time, unfortunately, one copy had been lost, and it just seemed to us all that there must be a larger audience, a larger appetite for people to read his book. In any case, even if not, it would be a wonderful thing to update the book, print more copies, and so, the idea for this book was born. We could correct the typos, add photos, and incorporate the poem. What a great project!

It struck me how Sal's attention to detail could be so vivid within his writing. He wrote about the people he met, their names, the places he had been to, the dates and times, in most instances some thirty years after these events had taken place. It was clear that there must have been some original journal he was pulling all this information from whilst writing his book.

Well, as it turns out, after a visit with my Nana Fay and perusing through all the old dusty stashed away family photos, I had inadvertently come across an extraordinary discovery, which had been completely unknown to anyone in the family, including my Nana.

What we had found, perfectly preserved within a large brown aged envelope, was Papa Sal's war diary! Covering his life day by day between the period 10th May 1940 – the 15th of August 1945. The problem was the whole thing was typed in Dutch.

Finding this relic so unexpectedly was truly an incredible shock. There were roughly 160 A4 pages of text, clearly all diary entries, covering the years 1940 – 1945, some with military codes and insignia, but this is all we could glean initially. The whole document would need to be translated from Dutch into English to reveal any true treasure that might lay within the entries.

Because of Sal, our family has strong roots in Holland, and it wasn't long after making this discovery that our Dutch relative Rika volunteered to take up the challenge. Carefully and diligently translating each entry and emailing the work over one or two pages at a time, day by day, the work was slowly being completed. We would be waiting patiently for the next batch to come through, like a photographer exposing a film in a dark room as the picture becomes gradually clearer. Soon we would have the entire thing, we just needed to be patient. It must have been tireless work for Rika to do, but a phenomenal effort on her part, which meant we had the entire diary translated within just a few months.

At the time, we did not know how historically significant this might be. We were unsure of the sensitivity of these documents or their implications. In any case, what a diary does for the reader like no other, is it puts you in the moment, almost like a time machine. Suddenly you get to experience a first-hand view of what it was like living through the war years, all from the perspective of a young sixteen-year-old migrant boy, who we see become a man.

So here it is now, all laid out for you to read and enjoy. Ode to Sal, 'Aim for the Top', Sal's Diary and many of my grandparents' most cherished photos of the time. Sal's story will take you on a rollercoaster ride of experiences, all of which are completely true and unedited. As you will read…

ODE TO SAL

ODE TO SAL

To My Wonderful Family, With Fondest Love, Dad

Are the words inscribed, on his book I've just read
Retelling life's story, ancestry and all
Losing a father young, meant standing up tall
Going to school, from the age of just six
Now living in Antwerp, the war in his midst
After two nights of bombing
The announcement was made
To leave Antwerp, only France would be safe
Destination was Roeselare, Sal cycled the whole way
Sal's Mother and Sister, however, would stay
The journey was fraught, sky bombers dived down
Machine guns pounding, thousands on the ground
Sal took cover in trench, he must lay in wait
Then rode and rode, with 'the lucky ones'

What would be his fate?
Pushbike, hitchhike, crossing the border to Boulogne
Train ride, Le Havre

Sky on fire!

As the bombing fell overhead again

Through serendipitous fortune, Sal made his escape

On the last boat to England, London his new landscape

A refugee, no English could speak

9 shillings, 7 pence (£ 0.48), the bike still at his feet

New job, Covent Garden, 1 pound a week

Grey flannel trousers are what he did seek

In the footsteps of his father, apprentice diamond cutter

An old family friend, this opportunity would lend

Then came that frightful night, which changed a lot of things

A land mine was dropped, Sal witnessed everything!

Stumbling through the rubble

Patrolling through the night

The worst air raid of the war so far

"Please turn off your light"

Early Spring 1942, Sal's 'Mother and Sister'

The word had got through

Both now arrested, sent to Internment Camps

Propelling Sal to now take his stance

Permission was given to join allied Air Forces

"Come back at eighteen and begin your courses"

R.A.F. pilot was not meant to be

The Royal Dutch Naval Air Service, Air Gunner was he

One week before passing, with fourteen Dutch lads

A training flight, would prove to devastate their lives

Three planes took off

Sal number two

Plane three would crash

A landing craft 'incoming' from out of the blue

Passing his wings, fly Mitchell Bomber

Missions complete

Top-class Air Gunner

Injured by shrapnel, in his upper right thigh

Landed, wounded

Sal had survived!

It wasn't long after

The war would be over

Finally reunited

Sal, his Sister and Mother

Duty done, life had begun

Korfball became a new passion

Captain of England, our first International

Dancing with Fay, feelings irrational

As the years flew by, struggle and strife

A dog called Sabre, two kids and a wife

Graft and perseverance would prove to endure

Sal had become a great entrepreneur

In the blink of an eye, retirement had come

A beautiful flat, which follows the sun

Sal's dreams had come true

Short memories are mine

Sadly, Sal died, I was fifteen at the time

So, this is his life story

Now for you to hold

'Aim for The Top'

A mantra to behold

See, we're ode to Sal

He's your Great Grandad

To My Wonderful Family, With Fondest Love, Dad xxx

AIM FOR THE TOP

AIM FOR THE TOP

My name is Sal Muller, born in Antwerp, Belgium, on the 16th of December 1924. I am the son of a South Africa born father, George Jacobus and a Dutch mother, Sophie Meijer and the grandson of Isidore Muller, a police officer in the Dutch Police force stationed in South Africa, champion of Holland and South Africa at Fencing, who was taken prisoner by the British in the Boer War and taken to a prisoner of war camp in Ceylon until the end of that combat. My grandmother, the wife of an officer, lived in Johannesburg and had three children there, my father being the oldest. When the war ended, my grandparents returned to Holland with their children. My father, having been born in South Africa, became a British subject by annexe.

In 1920, he married my mother in Amsterdam. By trade, he was a diamond polisher, a very good one, and because of that, my parents moved to Antwerp in Belgium, where my father made a very good living. Eventually, my sister was born on the 19th of August 1922, and I came along in December 1924.

My mother's father was also famous for different reasons. He had a kosher butcher shop in the heart of Amsterdam in Jordan Bree Street and was known for his salt beef sandwiches. People came from everywhere to purchase Meijer's sandwiches, just as they do from Blooms over here. Going through the phase of childhood, I went to school from the age of six. We were lucky enough to have a car in

1929, a Renault, which started with a handle, like the one used in films with the Bowery Boys.

At the end of the year 1930, my father left the diamond trade to start a butcher shop with a partner who sadly misfired over a period, I think about three years. He lost most of his money, became ill and sadly died on the 19th of June 1935, aged only forty. He was buried in a cemetery just over the border in Holland, a place called Puttee, and from then on, our lives changed.

My father had been a member of the Foresters organisation, and after my mother received a lump sum from them and used it to live on, things went backwards very steadily status wise, and so my sister and I would go after school to sell coffee and tea door to door as did my mother during the day.

When my sister was fourteen, she left school and went to Antwerp diamond cutters school to learn the trade. I stayed at school until that terrible day, the 10th of May 1940, when suddenly, in the early hours of the morning, I heard rumbling noises, aeroplanes and anti-aircraft gun sounds and the explosions of bombs. By air, we lived about one minute from the little airport of Deurne, just on the outskirts of Antwerp.

When it was time to go to school, I cycled all the way, which was daily anyway. It was about forty minutes from home as I went to the commercial school of Antwerp. At times I had to walk as we had no money to go by tram and then the journey there and back was two hours. When I arrived at the school, we were told that there was a war on and we should go home again. Nearby our school, there was a square called St. James Plein, and as I approached, soldiers were dispossessing bicycles for whatever use, so I quickly turned around and went through a back turning and home. What luck.

When I arrived, I carried my bike upstairs to the second floor where we lived as the old lady on the ground floor would not allow us to put the cycles in the hall. She was very house-proud. About 10:30 am, my mother and I went with a suitcase full of coffee and tea to the district where I was born. A few doors away from my very first home as a baby was a man who had a small warehouse from where he operated a wholesale business supplying beer to cafés and even the Antwerp prison. He said his assistant had reported to the army, and he could do with some help. He offered me twenty francs a day for two days. My mother told me to go ahead, so I helped this man Friday and Saturday. I earned real money for the very first time. I was fifteen and a half years old.

The bombers returned during the night for the first two nights, and on Sunday the 12th of May, an announcement was made that all men between the ages of sixteen and thirty-five would have to leave Antwerp towards France because it was rumoured that if the Germans reached our city, the men would be taken away to work in labour camps. Although I wasn't quite sixteen, my mother and I went to the local police station and asked for advice. Having had hard times during the last three years, I was older in my ways and mind, and the commissaire of police, an acquaintance of our family, told me to go. So, on Monday the 13th of May, I left on my bike and followed hundreds and hundreds of men and boys on the road to Roeselare in the Flanders towards France.

My mother had given me 100 francs to purchase whatever I needed. That was all there was. She had the 40 francs from me the day before as my wages. I had some money in a post office account, the money given to me on my 13th birthday a couple of years ago, but we couldn't get to that, as I left on my bike at 06:00 am. I kissed my mother and sister goodbye. We had no idea if we would ever meet again. I rode and rode just like everyone else and made towards Ghent. Before reaching Ghent, suddenly out of the sky, bombers dived down and used their machine guns on the thousands of people on the road. We threw ourselves in trenches, and when it was all over, quite a lot of people didn't get up anymore. They had been killed. I just cycled on and eventually reached Roeselare. When I got there, I was met with thousands and thousands of other people who had been told to go to the same town.

Nobody knew what to do with us, so the police advised us to move towards Ypres, the next town. The same thing happened there, and as I was drained, I noticed a school other people were heading inside, so I did the same and bedded down on the floor for the night and finished the sandwiches I had brought with me. Most of us travelled and crossed the French border the next day and rode towards Boulogne. We travelled through a small village and came across a bakery with a large queue of people. I joined the row and heard people say 'eight people', they were given a whole loaf. When it was my turn, I too said 'eight people' and got a loaf. That is all I had.

By now, I was in a small group of six people. A Dutch fellow Max Pels, whom I knew by sight from Antwerp and four other Belgian lads. Towards evening, roughly 20 km from Boulogne, we climbed a steep hill and found a hut-like AA box but a little larger. Whilst we debated to bed down, a lorry drove up the hill. I thumbed a lift, it stopped, and the driver took six of us with our bikes onboard and dropped us at some sort of barn where we slept in the hay surrounded by cow dung. We slept soundly that night as we were tired and decided we would go further the next day.

As we were in the town, I saw a friend of mine, Bill Boutelje, a committee member of the football club I played for 'Blue White' until the war started last week. He joined us, and we took a train further south. We reached a little place called Poix and were told that the train wasn't going any further, so we took to our cycles again on the way to Abbeville, where we caught a train to Le Havre. We were getting near that town when suddenly the sky lit up, and the Germans bombed Le Havre very heavily. We arrived in the middle of the bombing, and in the end, we were told to go to a school on the outskirts of the town where we were given some food from the Red Cross and had to stay the night. In fact, we stayed a few days in Le Havre.

Meanwhile, the Germans were advancing through France and were never far behind. On the 22nd of May, away from home for nine days, I met a Dutch family, the Gobitzs, whom I knew from Antwerp. They lived around the corner from us. Mr Gobitz was a corset manufacturer and supplier; he was with his wife and daughter. It was him who told me to try and get to England. He knew I had a British birth certificate. This was indeed correct. Although I was born in Antwerp, the children get their father's nationality, so Mr Gobitz took me to the British Embassy, where we were received with kindness. They gave me a ticket to leave Le Havre that night on the last boat to England. The Gobitz family said farewell, and Mr Gobitz even gave me 50 francs.

My own money had dwindled, and now I had 88 French francs altogether. That night the ship left at 22:00 pm, and we had a peaceful crossing to Southampton, where we docked early Wednesday morning. We were then vetted by immigration officials. I had to go back to the ship to get my bicycle as it was still on board. Eventually, we took the train to London, where we arrived at Waterloo station. From there, we went by red double-decker bus, which I had never seen to Norwood, where there was a receiving Centre for refugees in the Jewish orphanage. Once again, we were vetted, and our money was exchanged.

My 88 French francs became 9 shillings and 7 pence (£ 0.48), and so I had arrived.

I could not speak English at all, although I had learned at school for three years. My French was only fair, but I got by while in France. We stayed in the orphanage for several days, and then I was told I was to go to a hotel in South Norwood, the Beaulieu Heights. It was beautiful, and I even learnt to eat toast and marmalade, which I never knew before. I had my bike with me, and the first thing I did was go to the chemist shop opposite the hotel and buy a razor for 2/6. I had started to grow a beard. I was at the hotel for three days and was treated like a lord until a phone call came, instructing me to leave the hotel and make my way down to Brixton town hall.

With rucksack and bike, I made my way to Brixton, where I met a gentleman from the A.R.P., Mr Benavente. A violinist by trade, who played in an orchestra at the Strand corner house at night, but by day, was a volunteer helper for refugees. He spoke fluent Dutch and was married to a lady from Nottingham. We detoured to his home first to meet her and have some tea before going to my first proper address in England, 29 Grove Way, a turning between Brixton and the Oval, Kennington. There I met Mrs Williams, her husband and her daughter Phyllis, my new landlady. There were already seven refugees living there, six men from the Flemish part of Belgium, a town called Turnhout, and one boy aged about seventeen from the French-speaking part of Belgium Centre.

None of the men spoke English or French. The boy didn't speak Flemish or English, so within a very short time, I had become a sort of interpreter as I began to speak English. My English began to improve, and so did my French. As I started to speak English regularly, the grammar I learned at school began to help me. It wasn't very long at the house when I went for my first job and was interviewed at George Monro, one of the biggest fruiterers in Covent Garden. I was offered the job at £1.00 per week, which I accepted. I cycled to work a few times but then took the tram. Mrs Williams took 17 shillings out of my wages for food, £0.04 paid for insurance and six times a workman's return on the tram at 3p per day = 1/6 left me with 1/2 (one shilling and two pence (£ 0.06)).

I wore plus-four trousers, very smart, but people laughed at me, so I saved hard to buy a pair of long trousers, grey flannels. It took some months before I managed to save 5 shillings (£ 0.25) and bought them in Brixton Road second hand. I was very proud to be able to wear long trousers like other boys. I had no money to go out, so I had a hobby and studied the numbers of the buses and trams to see where they came from and went too. My first night out was with a young lady, Rose Ford. She worked for a florist and got two complimentary tickets for the Brixton Empire. I enjoyed the show, although I didn't understand any of the jokes. Later in the year, my wages were increased to £1.50 per week (Twenty-Five shillings).

The Germans began to bomb London regularly at the end of August, and things became difficult. Mrs Williams began to leave London quite often to go back to Wales, leaving us with bare rations to eat, and things became worse. Mr Benavente, with whom I had constant contact, asked his oldest daughter whether she would take me in as a young lodger. Her name was Kathleen Branson. She was married without children at that time to Alf Bransom, who was a full-time A.R.P. warden. They already had a young lad living there with them, his name was Sid, anyway, they decided that they would take a chance with me, so I moved in with them. They lived in Grove Lane, Champion Park, a few doors away from the Salvation Army Headquarters. I quickly got used to the new surroundings, the people, and soon after, I joined the A.R.P. as a messenger. Even though I was nearly sixteen, Mrs Bransom made me go to bed by 19:00 pm if I wasn't on duty at the A.R.P. post. She was very good but very strict.

As time went by, I met someone whom I knew from Belgium, and he told me that Bill Boutelje, whom I had said goodbye to in Le Havre, was in London working as a diamond polisher in Hatton Garden. This wasn't far from where I was working in Covent Garden. One afternoon, after work, I took a bus to Holborn and found the factory in Greville Street, Hatton Garden. Can you imagine the welcome I received when I entered the factory? There was Bill, the foreman who was a friend of my father many years ago, two more fellows whom I knew from Antwerp, one who lived in our turning when I was about eight. On Friday nights, my sister and I would go to his parents' and get sweets and peanuts. That was a treat. There were about eight workers in the factory, and before I left, they made a collection for me and asked if I would come again.

After a while, I paid another visit to the workshop and the foreman, who was a friend of my father in their heyday as polishers, offered me a job as an apprentice diamond polisher. Bill Boutelje would teach me, and my commencing salary would be £1.10 per week. I would also be the teaboy, fetching tea or coffee, rolls and sandwiches from the local deli. At the end of the week, I got tips which usually doubled my wages once I started. So financially, I improved a lot straight away, as I paid Mrs Bransom more money than when I lived with the Williams in Brixton. I steadily improved, and although I was not good at my job like my father was, I regularly got raises to improve my living standard.

Then came the night, which changed a lot of things. On the 10th of May 1941, exactly one year since the war started in Belgium, the German bombers came over and dropped a landmine that I saw coming down not far away from the house. The mine exploded and damaged all the houses, including ours. I walked through the rubble and started to look for Mr Bransom, who was on duty and would be in the street patrolling. I found him at the gates of Ruskin Park on his back, injured by the blast which knocked him off his feet. When the ambulance came, I accompanied him to the hospital at Kings College, which was only about 200 yards away and then went back to report the accident to Mrs Bransom, who was very upset. I then led the neighbours to the Salvation Army Headquarters, which was just up the road about 50 yards, where they were given shelter and coffee and food. They then stayed the night.

I went back on the streets patrolling right through the night. It was the worst air raid of the war so far. We lived in the damaged house for a while, and eventually, we moved to 45 Grove Park, a lovely big house. I then joined a local football team called Bromar and played regularly on Saturday afternoons during the winter. The raids had stopped for months, but there were no signs of the war ending.

In the early part of spring 1942, I had a letter from the Red Cross telling me that my sister had been arrested by the Germans and was sent to a concentration camp at Westerborg in Holland. Eventually, my mother was also arrested and sent there, and my sister was subsequently transferred to an internment camp in Germany, so I volunteered for the RAF. I wanted to be a pilot, and, on the 19th August 1942, I went to Cardington in Bedfordshire, where I had to do an entry exam. As I had not been to school in England, I sadly failed.

I came back to London and carried on working in the diamond trade. Meanwhile, I got in touch with the Dutch forces to see if I could join their Air Force. The Dutch government phoned the British government to find out if a British subject could join their combined forces. Permission was given for me to go in an allied Air Force. At the beginning of December, I was told to report on the 16th December, my eighteenth birthday, to the Dutch army at Marloes Road, Kensington, where I had to learn some basics before joining the Royal Netherlands Naval Air Service.

I was able to go home to Camberwell whenever I wanted for the first few weeks while awaiting my transfer. On 17th December, my second day in the forces, I went home to see Mrs Bransom, who had made me a birthday and farewell party for my friends and girlfriends. The mayor of Camberwell also came to wish me good luck. I left for Kensington with Mrs Bransom crying on the doorstep.

When I got to the Dutch H.Q. the next day, I was fitted out with an army uniform and told I could have the rest of the day and night off, so I went back to the Bransom's. Mrs Bransom was amazed to see me so soon. I stayed a few weeks in Marloes Road. One day there was a route march to Putney with full kit and rifle. I volunteered to peel potatoes instead, which was accepted, and I spent hours doing that while the other soldiers were away. After several weeks I had to report to the Dutch Navy H.Q. in North Row, Marble Arch, where they fitted me with a naval uniform. I became able seaman Sal Muller, no 90519/z.

They then gave me a train ticket to Morpeth in Northumberland, where I would learn to become an air gunner trained by the R.A.F. and, if I passed all exams, would join the Royal Dutch Naval Air Service. The course was to last six weeks. I did very well, scoring

84% on my first exam, a little less afterwards on the next two. There were 15 Dutch lads on the course, but sadly only 10 of us finished. On 29th March 1943, one week before our passing out parade as A.G.'s, an Air Vice Marshal visited the aerodrome to see how we were getting on. It was a cloudy morning, so usually, we wouldn't fly if the weather wasn't good, but because of the Air Vice Marshal's visit, we did fly.

We flew in the Botha aircraft, a twin-engine bomber used for training purposes. On board, there would be a pilot, an instructor and three trainee air gunners. I had just taken off in the second plane; the third plane took off and crashed into a craft descending to land from the previous training flight. Ten people died; five of the trainees were Dutch boys and one English; two of the dead were my roommates. We slept four in a room. It was very sad and disturbing. When the funeral of the ten who had died was held in the town's cemetery, the whole town seemed to be there. After the funeral, a young lady called Maureen, whom I had seen at the weekend dances, came up to me and asked if I had anywhere to go. I said no, so she invited me to go home with her, meet her parents and her brother Allen and have tea with them. I accepted and went to her home and stayed with the family until it was time to catch the last bus back to camp at 21:00 pm.

On 10th April 1943, we passed out as A.G's and got our RAF wing which I would wear on my RAF battledress, but we had our own wing with M.S. {Machinegun Shooter) on it. We then travelled to

London and then the train to Norwich, Norfolk. From there, we took a bus to our squadron at Attlebridge, 8 miles from Norwich, to join the 320 squadron, a Dutch outfit just learning to fly the Mitchell bomber B25, a twin-engine job that carried 8 x 500lb bombs.

On arrival, the commanding officer of A flight told me that my crew were on holiday, so I got seven days' leave as well. I went back to Norwich by bus, had a nice meal in a restaurant. The bill was 5 shillings (£ 0.25), the maximum one could spend in the war. At the restaurant, I met the owner Mr Levy. The restaurant was called The Curat House. He said, "Come and see me again next time you are in town". I went on to London and spent a lovely week there. On my way back, I went to Liverpool Street Station and saw a few pilots and navigators in Dutch uniforms go on the same train. One of the pilots was being kissed goodbye by a young lady for some time. When we arrived at Norwich, there was another young lady waiting for the same pilot, although I did not know this at the time but knew the next morning on parade when we got introduced. He was a man after my own style.

The squadron had only just been reformed. They were originally with Coastal Command bombing ships, and U boats and the aircraft used were Hudson's. Now we were training for land bombings, mainly in France. Our first important trip was on an air-sea rescue mission, and we found a dinghy not far from the Dutch coast with four American airmen in it.

We circled for hours around them. My wireless operator reported the position, and we hung around for nearly 6 hours until the rescue launch appeared. My WO was Jan De Jong; he was a very nice chap and came from the Dutch East Indies. We were in the air for 6 hours 15 minutes which was very long for the Mitchell due to its fuel consumption, but we made it back to base alright.

Time was going by, and we bombed towns and places in woods and forests, and the furthest we went inland was Fontainebleau. The raids were in broad daylight, but we had some fighter escorts high above us. We couldn't see them, but we knew they were there. We averaged about 12 000 feet high for our raids on targets.

On 27th November, I was on leave in London on my way to Morpeth, where I had not been since we passed out in April. With Bill Boutelje, my friend from the diamond polishing days and another friend Ronnie Davis, I went to a doctor's house in Stamford Hill, where Bill played some of his record collections for a young group of people. I met a nice young lady there. Her name was Joyce Kersh. She said I would meet her one day in London during my next leave.

On 4th December, I was promoted to Petty Officer. At the same time, my other roommate, who survived until now from Morpeth days, has been shot down over France. Hopefully, he and his crew have bailed out and taken prisoner of war. His name was Jan Kok, another East Indian lad.

On 15th December, I received a letter addressed from my sister delivered by the Red Cross informing me she was being transferred from the internment camp in Germany to a camp in Vittel in France.

On 29th December, I went to London and called the Kersh family in Hackney. Mrs Kersh opened the door and said, "My daughter Joyce is not here, but any friend of my daughter is a friend of the family." Mr Kersh said he would go and get Joyce as she was spending an evening with some of her friends not far away. I had a nice evening. Mrs Kersh made me some eggs and chips (eggs were rationed, I think about one a week). Later that evening, Mr Kersh and Joyce took me to the train at Hackney Down for me to return to Liverpool Street.

With D Day imminent, we made more raids sometimes twice a day and even three times. The third trip was at night and was frightening as you could see all the flak coming at you, and every tracer was the fourth bullet. Being over the target at night all on your own and the bomb doors open was no joke. After having made five trips in two days, once again, we had to go at night. Unfortunately, 320 squadron were to go in after two other squadrons, 98 and 180, went first. An aircraft dropping bombs every half hour meant by the time our aircraft was due to be over the target, it would be daylight, all on our own, and we would be a sitting duck for flak or fighters

I went to bed early evening at 20:15 pm and was woken up at 23:30 pm. I had a wash in cold water and prepared for the flight. We were supposed to take off at 02:00 am. I was so frightened, and I felt sure I would not come back. We were taxiing to the runway for take-off as the first two aircraft returned from France, they reported mist over the target area and so our trip was cancelled at the last minute for which I have been grateful all my life.

I got news from the Red Cross that my mother and sister were together in Vittell in the South of France in an internment camp and were being repatriated to England in exchange for German civilians to be flown back to Germany. I did not think it was possible in a war, but it was. The day they arrived in England, we made a bombing trip to France, and my other air gunner, Jimmy De Preter, a Dutch East Indian lad, black and with the most beautiful white teeth like pearls, was wounded. We had already been shot at by heavy flak on the way in, and after dropping the bombs on the way back, approaching the same position, my navigator Jaap Boom shouted, "We are near that flak point." Jimmy shouted, "Sir, I am wounded."

I was in the tail of the aircraft, undid my intercom and crawled away. Meanwhile, something seemed to hit my helmet; it was a piece of flak that bounced off. I managed to release Jimmy from the turret, lowered him on my lap and sat on the emergency exit door underneath the fuselage. We flew back like this all the way to England. Jimmy had been hit in the thigh, but the flak had travelled upwards through his intestine into his stomach, and he was in a lot of pain.

When we flew over the English coast, my pilot decided to fly to the nearest airfield and make an emergency landing. Sadly, it was like a potato field, and we were bouncing all the time up and down against the top of the aircraft, which did Jimmy no good at all. He was taken to hospital and died the next day. The very sad thing for me is that Jimmy had a military funeral. My crew and I could not go because we were on the battle order. As it was, we did not fly that day.

When back at our own airfield, I was given time off to go to welcome my mother and sister at the weekend for a couple of days. They had gone to Newton Abbott in Devon to stay with a second cousin of ours who lived there. He offered them a home for a few weeks so that they could acclimatise.

As the war carried on, my mother and sister came to London, and we found a flat to be shared with other people in the house in Highbury, North London. Then it happened, on the 11th of September 1944, we were to make a raid over Holland. Monday afternoon, we had to bomb the ferry boat which sailed between Flushing and Breskens. We made the trip, weather was good, but when we came over the target, we flew in a box of 6 aircraft. I flew number 2, the starboard side of the leading aircraft. The navigator in position 1 commanded, "Bomb doors open, bombing, bombing, bombing, bomb doors closed".

We had to fly around again as there was a little cloud over the target. The other 7 boxes of 6 bombers had dropped their loads. When we got over the target, we had lost height, and the anti-aircraft had us measured up and shot the lot at us. The bombs were dropped, and suddenly, I felt something warm along my right thigh. I had been hit by shrapnel. I shouted through my intercom, "Sir, I am wounded," unplugged my intercom and slowly forged myself along the fuselage towards the middle of the aircraft where I was calmed by my other gunner. We were heavily hit and managed to get back to base at Dunsfold in Surrey.

We were met by the squadron doctor and an ambulance and taken to a hospital in Horsham, Sussex. Mostly Canadian soldiers wounded in France were taken there. The doctor who operated on my leg was a Canadian, Dr Jones. He was marvellous. My mother and sister came to see me the next day. They had told my mother I had fallen off my bike.

I was in Horsham hospital for three weeks and then transferred to an RAF hospital at Halton in Buckinghamshire. I was there for two weeks and learning to walk again, I was limping a little, and then one of my many girlfriends, Mary Carrell, an Irish Naafi girl, came to visit me on Saturday, and we were allowed to go out for the first time since I was wounded. I did not have my uniform, so I borrowed a grey coat from a flight sergeant from New Zealand who flew with the RAF and was wounded. But he was about 6ft 3 inches, so the coat nearly touched my ankles. I am only 5ft 7inches.

We took a bus to Aylesbury and went to the cinema and saw Rita Hayworth in Cover Girl. Afterwards, we had something to eat, and I had to be back in hospital by 21:00 pm. Soon after, I was released from there and had 7 days' leave. Meanwhile, my squadron had moved to Melsbroek near Brussels, but I was not to return to the squadron. Instead, I was told to report to the Headquarters of the Royal Netherlands Navy Air Service at Marble Arch. I was told I had to make a card system about 320 squadron, their flying crews and their history from start to the present day and their experiences.

On the 1st November 1944, I was promoted to Chief Petty Officer and had to have a new uniform made at Aldgate Corner, Aldgate E.1. I was given an office of my own on the 6th floor at 2 Park Lane, a big building opposite Hyde Park Corner, just around the corner from Oxford Street. I stayed there when on 8th May 1945, the war in Europe came to an end. Not long after, the war with Japan was over after the allies dropped a couple of atom bombs on two big cities in Japan.

I was given permission to go to Holland to try and find any relations who had survived the war. I had lost over 70 family members in the concentration camps. However, my cousin Jaap and his wife Betty were found alive. They had been underground in Limburg with both their parents on a farm. My cousin and I had always been very close; he too was born in Antwerp in the same house as I, and his mother and mine were sisters.

I made the trip to Holland by motorboat from the Netherlands Navy, and we landed in Rotterdam harbour. From there, an army truck, about twenty of us, made our way slowly towards Amsterdam dropping off personnel on the way to Amsterdam, which made it very late before we arrived in the capital city. Jaap and Betty had a little flat at 1 Lepel Street, and when I rang the bell very late, they came rushing down the stairs to greet me. I hadn't seen them since 1939. Betty was Jaap's childhood girlfriend before the war. I had known her as well since I was about 12.

With me, I had a rucksack full of corn beef in tins, baked beans and other foodstuffs, bicycle tyres which were in very short supply still, cigarettes for exchange of goods when bargaining anything I might have wanted. I had a lovely week with them and with my aunt and uncle, who were also so lucky to have survived. I stayed in the forces until the 1st January 1946, when they demobbed me.

At first, it was difficult to settle down on civvy street. Meanwhile, my mother, sister and I had moved to Hackford Road, Stockwell, S.W.9, where we had a small self-contained flat in a house with two bedrooms. I went back to the diamond trade as a polisher, and my sister worked there as a diamond cutter.

During the early part of the summer, I read a story in the Evening News about a new game coming to England called Korfball. It is a game played by mixed teams 6 boys and girls, a kind of basketball-netball. I read the article with great interest as I knew the game from Antwerp before the war, and I had been a member of a club since I was 10. The club had no juniors. Only three of us were training with them every week. I had never played in league games before but was very experienced regarding the knowledge of the game and lots of shooting practice at the basket. At that time in 1946, there were only two countries playing Korfball, Belgium and Holland. It was introduced first in 1902 in Holland by a Dutch schoolmaster, Nico Broekhuizen. Later in 1923, it started in Belgium. The size of the pitch is the length of a small football pitch and the width about 45 yards, divided into 3 equal sections and a post with a basket (similar to a fruit basket from Covent Garden) 11 foot 8 inches high with no board behind the basket to help you.

The story about the game plus an address in Mitcham, Surrey was also in the paper, so I wrote, got a telephone number and met the gentleman who was a member of the Anglo-Netherland link up. I offered my help with the knowledge of the game, and on the following Sunday, I met the prospective playing members on Tooting Bec Common in Wandsworth, S.W.17. Some people had just returned from Holland, where they went for a course to learn the game. So straight away, they welcomed me, and I started teaching the game immediately from what I remembered, what I had learnt as a boy in Antwerp.

The club was formed and called Wandsworth KC, but as we had no opposition as we were the first club, we trained regularly every Sunday morning, and at the end of the training session, we had a little game among ourselves. It was very difficult to keep the interest going without a proper game. Meanwhile, there was another schoolmaster with his assistant who started the second team in Croydon, Mr Wallbancks, with his assistant Miss Davies. Our first match was then arranged to be played between Wandsworth and Croydon on a very nice pitch in Upper Norwood. Strangely enough, the pitch was about 500 yards away from the hotel where I first stayed when I arrived in 1940.

On the Saturday evening before the match, I had gone to a dance at the Astoria dance hall in the West End, in Charing Cross Road. A nice young lady stood in front of me, and I asked her to dance. She accepted, and then I noticed how pretty she was. I told her my name, and she told me hers. We danced all evening, we had orange juice upstairs, and after the dance was ended at 23:00 pm, I said I would like to take her home. She agreed, but she lived in Dalston, EB. We took the bus to Ridley Road, where she lived, and I took her to the top of her road and planned to see her in the West End the next day to take her to the cinema to see Black Narcissus[4], a film with Jean Simmonds and Stuart Granger. When I arrived home later that evening, I had to get back from Dalstonto Stockwell. My mother and sister were already in bed awake as I hadn't arrived home earlier as usual. I told my mother that I had met the girl I was going to marry. Her name is Fay. It didn't please my mother at all, and then I went to bed.

On Sunday, I went to Piccadilly Circus, outside the Trocadero restaurant, to wait for bus 38 to arrive from Dalston. Fay was nicely on time and looked lovely in a green tweed suit, stockings with seams and nice brown shoes. When Fay told me her name was Fay Solomon, I thought her father must be that fishmonger and boxing promoter who had a fish shop in Ridley Road. I thought I was set up for life. However, it was only a coincidence that the surname was the same. In fact, Fay's father had died the year before. Anyway, we went to the Strand corner house, where we had some tea, and Fay ordered toast, in case I couldn't afford more. Then we went to Leicester Square to see the film which was good.

I had borrowed my mother's chocolate coupon and bought a bar of Bourneville to eat during the performance, but it was I who had nearly all of it, as she wasn't that keen. After the film I took Fay to a restaurant in Charing Cross Road, had a meal and I proposed to marry her perhaps sometime during the next year. She said she would think it over. It was rather sudden. I took her back to Dalston E8 and, when I left her, decided to see her the following night to take her to the first Korfball match in England. We made a time to meet at Tottenham Court Road underground station but didn't state which exit. Fay worked as a sales lady at D.H. Evans, and I worked around the corner from the factory in Greek Street, W.1. Time was getting on, and Fay hadn't arrived; I finally found her at one of the exits. We rushed on the underground to the Elephant and Castle and then took a 68 bus to Norwood. We managed to get to the match with little time to spare, the game was a great success, and we won 16-1. We had teas afterwards in the pavilion, a few speeches and congratulations for our play and my teaching, then we left as Fay had a long way to go to Dalston. I took her as far as the Elephant and Castle and put her on the 35 bus to take her home and made my way back to Stockwell by underground.

In June, we had our first team over from Holland to play Wandsworth on Tooting Bec Common. It was a team from Schiedam. We played on the inside of the running track and it was a success. The Dutch team beat us 3-4, which was a very good result for us.

Life went on in the usual way, and when Fay's sister Ray married Hymie in January 1948, I was asked to be the best man. We then arranged to get married ourselves and settled for the 29th of August.

In April, London played Sheffield at Korfball in Derby, which was won by London 3-1. Of the two teams, 12 players would be selected to play Holland B at Sheffield. I was one of the selected 12 and made captain of England in the first international. I was very proud. We played in May against the Dutch and lost 2-7. We were heavily outclassed.

The London Korfball Association was formed in July 1948, and I was present as a founding member. I was made the first match secretary. My team Wandsworth won the championship. There were only 4 teams, a 3rd and 4th club formed, Bee and Mitcham.

Fay and I were married in the Brixton synagogue, Effra Road, S.W.2, on a Sunday afternoon

We went to Brighton for a week's honeymoon and stayed our honeymoon night at the Grosvenor Hotel, Victoria. The following day, we went to Brighton by train. We stayed at the St. Albans Hotel, Regency Square. It was near the West Pier. £7.70 per week. The next morning my mother appeared for breakfast to see us. Although her English was poor, she managed to get to Brighton, and by asking and whatever, she found the hotel. She stayed with us all day, and in the evening, Fay and I took her back to Brighton station to the train to take her back to London. When we came back from our honeymoon, we moved in with my mother and sister for a few weeks.

We then took a couple of rooms with an aunt who lived in Brent, N.W until eventually, we got a flat in a house in Plaistow, East London, E.13. next door to Fay's eldest brother Alex and his wife, Kitty. Things were tough, and we had no way to make money. We paid 13/- (£0.65p) per week rent, which was cheap enough, and then, in the early part of spring, Fay became pregnant. Sadly, due to the recession time in the diamond trade, I was put off for some time and looked for a job and started work for a while at John Lewis in Oxford Street, but the wages were poor, £5.15 per week.

On 11th December, our son Geoffrey Neal was born in St. Mary's hospital at Stratford, E.15. In May of this year, I captained England again against Belgium at Woodford, and we lost 3-9. Under my captaincy, Wandsworth A became champions for the second time. In 1950 I captained England again against the Dutch, and we lost a very good game 2-4. In 1951, I captained against Belgium and lost 4-11 at Hounslow. This year my daughter Hilary was born, and so now we had two children and were delighted that our little family was complete.s

I had been in the diamond trade for some time and bad times came back again. I decided to try my luck at something else and went on the road as a rep. I bought a paper called The Grocer, and in the adverts column, there was one that might be it. The company called M. Pearl Ltd supplied groceries to the small grocer shops and sold sweets from Sweden that were not on the rationing system. I phoned the company and got an interview. They were in Euston Road, London, N.W.1. I impressed the directors, and they offered me a job as a rep at £7.00 per week and £1.00 for expenses. I used my bike to save money from my wages which were low. I travelled through all weather conditions. I opened a lot of accounts, but things were very difficult with two children as well.

To make things easier financially, I started to sell DOVE polish door to door. It wasn't easy, but it helped. When Geoffrey's first birthday came along, I went to a new block of flats over Canning Town bridge. First turning left, they had built a brand-new block of flats—nine-storey high. There were ninety flats, so I took the lift to the top floor with two heavy bags full of tins of polish, 3 sizes and told the ladies this was the polish that these special floors required, and they didn't smear. I sold 55 tins that day and came home when the party was over, the family had enjoyed it, and I was able to pay for the expenses.

This year I was selected to play for England against Holland in Rotherham, and we won for the first time by 7-3. I was delighted. I changed clubs and joined Mitcham K.C. They made me captain, and we won the championship two years running. I did think it was time to get my own team formed, and so I started West Ham K.C. in 1953. I changed my job and became a rep with William Blake, also in the grocery trade, still on the bike; I couldn't drive anyway at that time. One evening in May, I fancied going dog racing and went to West Ham greyhound track with just £ 2.00. I played numbers 1 and 2 reversed, which cost 4 shillings (20p)

The first race 1-2 came up and paid £6.00, the second race it came up again and it payed £1.20. I lost the next two races and went home with the winnings and decided to start driving lessons which I took at 15/ [75p]- per hour and learned to drive in 15 lessons, I passed first time. That was probably the best money I ever spent.

West Ham K.C. was progressing with difficulty. We had a job getting people to travel over the water to places like Tooting, Mitcham and Croydon; no one had a car. On the home ground, we couldn't get a pitch to play on Sundays. After one season, we were forced to fold up because of a lack of members. We had won 8 matches and lost 3, I sold all the equipment to other clubs, and with the money we received, we ended up in front with £ 14.30, so I split up the money and sent £5.50 to the cancer fund, £5.50 to the TB fund and £3.30 to the local blind association at West Ham. I stopped playing for a couple of seasons. I was so disappointed.

In 1955 I applied for a job with Lipton Ltd, grocery wholesalers and got the job with them at £4.00 per week plus commission and a little black Ford car. That was an improvement to the bike. The area they gave me was in the West End. I had W.C.2 area and Victoria S.W.1. I was pleased with my job and tried very hard to make new customers, which I did very well. Financially I had improved, but I needed more money for the clothing and school for the children. So, I decided to get a second job. I started working part-time as a waiter for a catering firm in Knightsbridge that specialised in debutante balls and big dances attended by the Royal family. Princess Margaret was often at all these kinds of parties, and I served Gary Cooper, the American film star and other famous people. Often, I worked right through the night, sometimes as late as 05:00 am, before I went home to bed for 3 hours and back on the road for my company, although it was just once a week.

One day, one of the restaurants I supplied for Lipton, the Omelette Bar in Lisle Street, asked me if I could help part-time. I gratefully accepted and worked there on Monday, Wednesday and Saturday nights. On Saturday, it was from 17:00 pm until 02:00 am. This lasted some months, but then in 1956, we had trouble with the blockade of the Suez Canal in Egypt. We couldn't get petrol easily, and it was rationed. I had to give up my part-time job, which I really liked. However, I got promoted by Lipton, and they gave me the East End of London and Essex, so I progressed a little.

A few months ago, I opened an account in Kahn's restaurant opposite the Regent Palace hotel. The owner said to me, "I know you." It was Mr Levy, the man who opened that restaurant, The Court House, which I visited in 1943 when I was an air gunner. We had a chat, and he asked me if I would like to become his manager in his restaurant. I refused but said I would not mind working there part-time a couple of nights a week. He agreed, I started, but it didn't last very long. He was possessive and, at times, difficult.

My area in East London and Essex became better, I opened more accounts, and the repeat business improved. One day I called West Ham Stadium, where the dog racing took place twice a week. They had stock car racing once a month and a speedway in the summer. I met the manageress from the restaurant, Mrs Stevenson, who was an ex Australian speedway rider's wife. She was very nice, and I explained why I had come. She said she was satisfied with her present suppliers but took my name and address in case she changed her mind. I mentioned I worked part-time as a waiter. Should she ever need one, I would like the job. I only lived 10 minutes away at Plaistow.

A short while later, there was a phone call for me. Fay took the message, "Would Mr Muller call at the West Ham stadium whenever possible." It was Wednesday evening, so the next morning, I went to the stadium, asked for Mrs Stevenson, expecting to get my opening order for Lipton. However, it was not for the order she had phoned. She wanted to know if I had any experience as a wine waiter. I said no but was willing to learn. She told me to come on Friday evening for the dog meeting and Saturday evening for the speedway. "I'll put you on trial; if I like your work, you stay; if not, you'll have to leave". I stayed nine years. Having progressed from waiter to wine waiter, eventually, I bought a beautiful second-hand red coat so that I could reach the top in that field by being a toastmaster. I did my first job at that in the early 60s and did quite a few jobs at charities for nothing, just the honour and helping organisations and people worse off than ourselves.

I was Toastmaster at the wedding of Alan Sealey, outside right at West Ham F.C. Four days after the wedding, Alan played against Bayern Munich and scored both goals in the 2-0 win. I was also the Toastmaster at the wedding of Charly Gray, amateur England footballer at inside right who played for Leytonstone.

In July 1957, there was a competition for the chairman's prize for the rep who produced the best results for the company over a period of three months. At a lunch reception at Cheeseman's of Lewisham, the chairman Mr Spinks made a speech and said that the rep who did the best for the company, including opening new accounts, would earn £50. prize and hoped that this rep would buy premium bonds with it. He then called out the winner, and to my surprise, I had won it. I duly bought the bonds with the voucher.

In 1958, due to a lack of trade and heavy pilfering by drivers and their mates, Lipton decided to call a halt to the wholesale department side. I was offered a special job by the company pioneering a brand of tea not known called Doctor Tea. They wanted me to supply the grocer shops all over North and East London with a van, selling direct. One other rep would get the same job covering South and West London. My wages would be the same as I finished when we packed up and would be guaranteed for 12 months, hoping to get the brand famous like Lyons and Brooke Bond. I didn't fancy the challenge, declined the opportunity and left. I joined a small catering firm called Salix Provisions, owned by two brothers who supplied a lot of little cafes with catering goods. I was made many promises, but they didn't materialise, so in 1960, I decided to leave them for a new venture.

I had a friend Mr Ernie Swithenbank whom I had known since 1952 when I had worked part-time for his company selling Dove polish door to door to help my income. His company called English Waxes, needed reps for London and Essex to sell polish to the grocery trade. I accepted and started at £10.00 per week plus commission. It wasn't easy at all, but I had a job, a new car, a Morris Minor and I had my little job at the stadium. So, we managed. It was time we made a move and started to look around for a house. We found a little semi-detached house at Elm Park, Essex, near the doctor, the trains, the school and shops, all within literally yards. The price of the house was £3400.00, and so we paid a deposit of £1500 and hoped to pay the balance as soon as we could.

Eventually, my company was sold us out to a Kiwi polish company, and I was out of a job. I took a job with a smaller firm but did not feel confident the product was good enough, so I made the decision to quit. What was I to do for the future? Fay was working as a manageress in a gown shop in East Ham. Her boss owned some new shops on the side turning, and he offered us one. And so, we started a little cafe. The place was very small, room for about 15 people. We had bars made and bought 15 stools, 5 on one side, 5 opposite and three at the window. There was not much room for cooking, so we didn't make chips, mostly rolls and sandwiches, hot soup and any kind of omelettes. We opened it, and on the first day, we made £3.76. I made a note on the wall that any old age pensioner would get one penny off a cup of tea

The next morning, we arrived at the shop a fraction late because of the traffic, and outside the cafe, there were about 120 people queuing. I thought they must have heard about the penny off. I told Fay we are late, and I must put the urn on first, with no rolls or sandwiches ready. We quickly opened the cafe, did the right things, but only a couple of people came in to find out if we had any cigarettes. Apparently, they were not waiting for us but for the Grey Green buses which took these people to the seaside, outside our cafe was where they got on. It wasn't funny at the time, although it seems like that now.

Anyway, we weren't a success, so I decided that I would like to do some selling of some kind. I bought a second-hand car for £250, a little ford estate, and on Thursdays when we shut at 13:00 pm. I would go out and sell hair lacquer, toothpaste, and several lines to shops all over the place. It went pretty well, and the time came. I had to make my mind up to sell the business and concentrate on making a living selling full time. I didn't think I could do it, but Fay was optimistic and said, of course, you can, so we put the cafe up for sale. After a few weeks, a man came along and liked what he saw, we had a few customers having omelettes, and he came back the next week, and again we were busier than before. He had a workman's cafe and found it too much, so we sold it, and although we made very little overall, we got out in time. Sadly, within months the man died as he had a tumour on the brain.

I bought my first new van, an Austin A55, and loaded it with more lines called at more shops and districts further apart. I called on the shops, took the order, went back to the van, assembled it, delivered it and took my money, and made my way to the next shop. On Tuesdays, I started going to the country, so I made four weekly journeys, one to Luton, one to Harlow, one to Southend, and one to Chelmsford. I started buying from manufacturers and having deliveries made to Elm

Park, where we had a little outhouse at the back of the garden and a shed made of wood built next to our garage.

Earlier in the year, I had received a letter from the secretary of the Bee K.C. to take the first team over as captain so that perhaps we would win the korfball cup final, as we had in the past two years, we had been in the final but lost. I accepted the position, changed the team around, split my male partner with the ex-captain in my division, and we played and won the final by 7-5 on a windy afternoon at Clapham Common. It was my first cup winners medal. I was also honoured for the first time to referee the fourth-coming international between England- Holland B. It was a great feeling. Soon afterwards I went to Amsterdam to be taught refereeing at the top level for one week.

In June of that year, Bedford brought out a new van. We exchanged our Austin A55 for a Bedford. I had more room and so could take more goods on board. We had shelves put up inside so that the smaller products would not get damaged. The years passed on perhaps with not a lot to mention, except that business was alright. I bought a bigger van in December 1966, a new ford six-wheeler, the first off the assembly line. I had alarms put on it, and just before the second lot had to be put on, the van was stolen out of the garage where I parked with all the goods on board. It was the 4th of January, the amount on board was worth about £1700.00. I had a tough time working only with the car while they were looking for the van.

We got ourselves a puppy Alsatian to protect us from having further burglaries. The man who was supposed to put the second alarm on the previous week said he was unable to do it, so we had to wait another week. That Friday evening, Fay, the puppy Sabre, and I put the van away late after coming from the stadium, and I noticed a green Morris Oxford car in the driveway past my van with a GB plate in the middle of the boot uncommon.

There was condensation on the rear window, so I assumed there were people inside but didn't write the number of the car down nor the letters. We went home, and I came back in the morning to take the van to the man who was supposed to put the second alarm on. I saw straight away that the garage doors had been tampered with and, by uplifting the doors, saw that the van had disappeared. All the goods on board, what a tragedy.

I went to the police at Hornchurch, explained everything but had no proof. I had no record of the number plate. They couldn't do anything. I knew a man who had some of my goods in his shop in Green Lanes, Ilford; there were blue paint marks on some of the items of lines that had disappeared. I didn't have the guts to tell the police in case of reprisals.

On a Sunday morning, I had my first match against a team in Edmonton. I had the children with me and waited outside the shop in case the guy opened. He didn't so I went to the match which we won, and I scored a hat-trick. On Tuesday, I served the Southend area. I went to a garage in the town where the man worked who was supposed to have put my alarm on the van (the second one), and to my amazement, a green Morris Oxford was parked on his premises with GB plates in the middle of the boot. I went to the police in Southend. I knew Inspector Poole there. He saw me but couldn't help.

I worked from the car as the van had not been found, after about four weeks, somebody phoned me from Colliers Wood in S.W. London, who had this new van outside his house all that time and finally looked inside, found my order books with my address and all they had left in goods were baby pants maybe because the make was not so well known. The back-door handle had been forced. The man told me he had told the police many weeks ago that the van was outside his house and, in total, had made three phone calls to them. When I complained to the police about this, they told me that the man had no right to phone and tell me what had happened.

By now, I had to employ assessors to try and claim from my insurance company. They finally paid me about £1200 but had to pay the company an additional 5% for handling my affairs. I had to find a new place for my van to be garaged. I couldn't leave it at Park Lane anymore, and at last, I found a place more secure inside a garage at Rainham. The owners were two brothers named Wall & Co. They were very kind to me, and they charged me only £2 per week. Each day I did the journey from Elm Park to Rainham and back to leave the van there at night. Besides travelling all day, it was challenging and selling and replacing the goods at night. However, we carried on, and then I bought a bigger van, a two-ton Comer.

Geoffrey, my son, was by now working with me. He was seventeen. He had tried a job in the city in a stockbroker's firm, didn't like it, and asked Fay one night to ask me if he could come and work with me. Of course, I agreed, and it helped quite a bit.

The big van was completely fitted out with proper shelves, and I was able to walk inside without bending down. Time went by, and sometime later in 1971, I went to a wholesaler on a Friday in Hackney. I liked his warehouse. It was big, so there was plenty of room. The man's name was Dave Miller. I said, "you know what Mr. Miller, I could do with your warehouse" he replied, "you want my warehouse, you can have my f~#/?*# warehouse". I asked him what he wanted for it. There was only a short lease, approx. Twenty months, but it was a start, I thought. He wanted £1000 for the lease. The rent was only £20.00 per week. He said he would sell me his trolleys, his Transit six-wheeler van, and remaining stock, whatever I required. I said I would like to talk it over with Fay first.

I phoned her from the office and told her the situation. She thought it would be fine. We had money in the bank we did not use much for our own use, and it would give us a chance to improve our living status to move from Elm Park one step up one day soon. Fay came down to Hackney by train and bus, liked it, and we made a deal with Mr. Miller. There was a fellow who lived next door who was a driver for him, and he was available if required to work for us. We were able to move in soon after all the legal work was done. It was now about the beginning of 1972. Businesswise as a cash & carry, we did not improve at all, even I had hoped it would. Customers previously served by Mr. Miller did not find us cheap enough and so all the customers he had we lost straight away. It didn't matter much as I had my own runs and own customers, but at least now we had a base to work from.

On the 10th of December, we decided we would look around to find a new place to live as a reward for all the hard work we had done over the years. We went to an estate agent in Hainault to look at a house, but it wasn't big enough. I needed space for a van if possible. However, the van was big enough and the place big enough to go inside the warehouse. I said to Fay perhaps we should try Gidea Park, which is a lovely area near Romford and not too far away from Hackney. We had the dog also and needed to be near a park for exercise and whatever else. We went to Main Road Gidea Park to an estate agent, and as it happens, there was not a lot available at the time. The agent said I have only two properties not far away in the price range you mentioned you could afford.

One is a house, Spanish style, the other a bungalow. It wasn't far away from the office and near the park. We went in his car, and it was a long road alongside the Gidea Park golf course and seemed a long walk. I said I thought it was too far when I saw the house. He said in that case, the bungalow was also too far, and as he got to the park, he turned left and took us back to the office. We left there a bit upset, and then we were going to see a house the next day in Hainault on the borders of Chigwell. Again, it was too small, so we decided to have another look around Gidea Park.

We started from the Main Road in Gidea Park and went along the park, turned left as the road went left, and finally landed at the same spot where we were the day before, turned left into the turning, and on the corner of that turning stood a beautiful bungalow completely detached with beautiful flower beds. I stopped the car and said to Fay, "have you still got the details from yesterday"? She said yes, and when we looked at the address, it was 2 Nether Park Drive, the actual bungalow.

It was nearly 14:00 pm, and we had a function to go to in Stoke Newington, N.16 by 16:00 pm. The details didn't have a phone number, so I said, "let's take the bull by the horns and ring the bell". The price was £14,000. I got out of the car and rang the bell. A pleasant man opened the door. "Sorry to bother you, sir, is this bungalow for sale?" He said, "yes, it is. My wife and I are having a bite to eat. Come in and look around yourselves, and we'll join you in a few minutes". We started in the front, where there were two bedrooms, one on each side of a long corridor. The one on the right was the main bedroom, very nice. The second one was very similar but had terrible wallpaper, very dark. Then next to the main bedroom was a smaller bedroom, next to that was the bathroom which was beautiful. It also had a mirror and a light above it. Across was the lounge very nice except it was not as big as I would like a lounge. It was 15x12 feet, with a middle door leading to the garden.

Then we saw the kitchen, which also had a door leading to the garden from the side. The garden at the front was colossal and at the back also. There was room at the side where we could have double doors fitted to the road so we could put the big van behind it so as not to upset the neighbours. There was also a brick-built air raid shelter which could be used as a lovely shed. The garage was away from the bungalow to the left. The plot was 116x108 feet and 60 feet across, completely detached, with the bungalow in the middle.

Fay and I looked at each other. We knew it was for us. We started talking with the owner Mr. Birchley who said a young couple with their little baby had called a while earlier and were impressed and intended to place a deposit with the agent. We said we would make our minds up right away. We could see the potential of the bungalow and agreed to the price with the vendor. Providing the young couple had not been before us to the agent. We would place a deposit the next morning at 09:00 am.

We went home happy, smiling, and full of it. We had a bath and dressed for the party where we arrived at 17:00 pm. We told the family we had seen a lovely bungalow which we hoped to buy the next day. After the party, which was after midnight, we went home via the bungalow at Gidea Park and noticed how dark it was. The streetlight on the corner of the turning obviously goes out after midnight. We then made our mind up that if we bought the bungalow, one of the first things we would have done was to install floodlights. We went home. We were tired but had a very satisfying day. We slept well that night, and in the morning, Fay went to the estate agent and put the deposit down to buy the house, where we would spend the next 16 happy years.

Hilary had already married earlier in the year, so the two bedrooms we had plus the smaller one, we made into a lovely dining room. We put our house up for sale on a Friday. Our advert in the evening paper appeared early the next day, and within a short time, we had phone calls, and a young Scottish lad said I'm coming down and want it. The price we asked for was £9000.

We had the three-day week and electricity cuts, and when the fellow arrived, the lights were out. He liked what he saw by candlelight and gave us a cheque as a deposit. We had six people see the house. They all wanted it. Some young lady wanted it for her parents and found it so easy near all facilities and offered us more money, but we wouldn't do that as we had taken the deposit from the lad. Altogether we had 76 telephone calls. It wasn't long before we moved to Gidea Park.

Business was not good in the warehouse, still the 3-day week. Meanwhile, our son-in-law Harvey had joined us as a driver. In June,

I felt I needed a rest and went on my own to Rimini, Italy, where I stayed at the Grand, a very nice hotel. I had bought a tennis racket and learned to play. I hired the court for an hour and played the ball boy, who was about 14 years old, and he beat me. The next day I played a game with another boy of about ten and managed to beat him, so I improved during my stay. At the end of the week, I was asked to play with other guests in the hotel. On Friday, there was a tall Dutchman who challenged me to a game on Saturday, but I had already made arrangements for the morning. Not to disappoint him, I said I would play him late afternoon. I won both matches and was thrilled.

When I came back from holiday, I felt more relaxed and decided Fay ought to have a holiday soon too. Fay decided she would visit my sister in Tel-Aviv for ten days. We applied for tickets, and she was to travel on the 5th of October from Heathrow. The tickets arrived relatively late on Thursday, literally the day before the flight. Friday morning Geoffrey and I took her to the airport early due to the important Jewish holiday Yom Kippur started Friday night. She arrived in Israel safely in the afternoon.

On Saturday, the 6th of October, we had the biggest Korfball tournament ever in this country, between Belgium, Holland, and England. I went to the matches, and afterwards, I took some of the Belgian officials to their hotel at Victoria before going home to my bungalow. I got home about 19:00 pm. Straight away, the phone rang. It was Hilary telling me that Israel was at war. They had been invaded.

They were unexpectedly attacked by the Arabs on a holy day when most people were attending synagogue for prayers. She said to try and call Mum back. I tried all evening to phone Tel-Aviv but couldn't get through.

Roughly 02:00 am in the morning, the operator here managed to get a phone call to Tel-Aviv, where everything was calm, and I spoke to Fay, my sister, and brother-in-law. On their way to the synagogue that morning, the sirens suddenly went off at about 09:00 am, which meant an attack was taking place. Everybody started running about, and some of the younger men were rushed away to go home, put on their uniforms and report to their units. It must have been chaos. Fay promised me she would try to get back as soon as possible.

On Sunday, the Korfball tournament between the three countries was continued with the final between Belgium and Holland at Tooting and Mitcham football ground. It was a great match, and the TV cameras were there as well for the first time.

On Thursday of this week, Fay came back from Israel. A friend of my brother-in-law pulled a few strings and managed to get her a ticket to return to England earlier than planned. We were pleased she was back, and meanwhile, she had lost 6 pounds in weight. Geoffrey then suddenly decided he wanted to go to Israel and work on a Kibbutz, volunteering with the harvest. He booked his flight and went. We were left one man short in the warehouse, but my brother-in-law David, Fay's brother, whom we had given some space in the warehouse to start his own business in cutting and designing, had a son who had no job. He started to work with us for a certain period on a temporary basis. John, who lived next door to the warehouse, was still with us. He also had the keys to the place to open, so if the alarms went at any time, we wouldn't have to come all the way from Gidea Park. So good for security, we thought.

To open or shut the warehouse, one needed to know a code name, usually one word. However 'Granley', our alarm company, agreed to the request that I could have a 2-word code. I wanted it to be the "Mitchell Bomber", the aircraft I flew during the war. As time went by, I noticed or imagined that my stock was going down, and the sales had not improved. I said to Fay, looking at the stock. They seem low. Maybe there is something wrong. I phoned Granley and asked if ever 'Mitchell Bomber' ever opened at the weekend. They said they would look at the records and let me know. They came back an hour later and said that for two consecutive weeks, the warehouse was open between 09:00 am and closed again at 12:00 pm. I was shocked but knew that my instincts were right.

I spoke to John the next morning, and he was cross and denied it. He said he would sue the company and me. He phoned them had words with them and after two days Granley came back to me and said there was a mistake and whoever had said that the warehouse was open on those days had been sacked and left the company already. John then left our employ, and we carried on as well as possible. The council, meanwhile, kept asking us to leave as they did not want to extend our lease. Soon after, one of our reps came for an order and asked me if I knew that a warehouse was for sale in Plaistow, E13. Right opposite Plaistow library in North Street.

As it happened, I had seen the board outside the place only recently, and so I got in touch with the agents. The premises were freehold and belonged to a wholesaler in tobacco and sweets who had sold out to a bigger company called Palmer & Harvey. I went to see the warehouse liked it but thought it was a little small. However, we did not have many options, so I bought them. We had brand new alarms installed, we had a sitting tenant upstairs who had their own flat and door entrance, and she paid £2.00 per week rent. The flat was self-contained.

It seemed a little extra from a security point of view. The area was also nearer to Gidea Park. We still had our dog Sabre, but she was getting difficulties with her legs, she was a little overweight, and it affected her legs. She had been doctored as a puppy. I had taken advice from the vet surgeon at West Ham dog stadium about it and was told it would have no effect later in life, but it did.

Geoffrey came back from Israel and started mini cabbing. He didn't particularly want to come back to us. He did this for some months, and one day a week, he used to help us out. He did this for some months, and the minicab firm told him to get a car with four doors and not two as it was. He didn't like that and so with the advice of our accountant Mr. Taylor, he came back to us working full time. Sabre, meanwhile, wasn't too well, and we took her to the Vet Hospital in Wanstead, where she stayed till the weekend. After three days, when we collected her, she was full of life as she was years ago, but it was for a short while. She had to have golden injections, and as there would be side effects, it was only a matter of days before she started to lose control of her water. Geoffrey and Fay then took her to the vet and had her put down. They hadn't told me. When I came home, I was told the news and was very upset. We buried her at a dog's cemetery in Waltham Abbey, Essex.

On the 19th of March, Hilary gave birth to our first grandson. His name is Darren, a lovely little boy and ever so blond. Meanwhile, that same day as my mother-in-law's 97th birthday and we threw a surprise party at home in Gidea Park for her. She knew nothing about it. My brother-in-law David, sister-in-law Ray, her son, and David's wife Shirley fetched her from her home. When they arrived, I said to my Mother-in-law, hello, Mum "you didn't tell me you were coming. Fay and I are going to a dance later". She said, "it doesn't matter. If you give me a cup of tea and I have seen you both, I am satisfied". When she came into the lounge, friends and family were all there waiting to greet her, with so many gifts and presents. Her face lit up, and it took a few moments for her to realise all this was for her. It was such a success. I decided to do it each year until she reached 100 and hired a hall. Unfortunately, it was not to be, and in April of that same year, she suffered a slight heart attack. She did get through it for a short while.

Now in bed at home, she watched the cup final between West Ham and Fulham, which West Ham won quite fortunately 2-1. On Sunday, Fay and I went to see her, and she said after greeting me, "you know you were lucky yesterday. Fulham should have won". I had been to the match. I said to her, "Mummy, don't get cocky with me. I'll be in bed with you in a minute", and she replied, "what can you do for me at my time of life". We left her quite happy but sadly, the next day, she deteriorated and, in the evening, closed her eyes and passed on peacefully. She was the most wonderful person who never said anything wrong about anyone. I missed her then as I miss her now. She was truly great.

Nothing exciting happened for a couple of years, then Geoffrey met Marilyn, and they decided to marry in June 1976. Meanwhile, one day I had been to Luton, my eyes were sore and tired. I decided to see an eye specialist. He told me that there was nothing wrong. Did I have any other symptoms? I said no, except I drink a lot of coca-cola. He then said, maybe you have too much sugar. I hoped not, but at the same time, I made an appointment to see an old doctor in the East End who used to look after my wife Fay when she was a little girl and the rest of the family. I had to wait in a cold waiting room, and when he was free with the patients who were seen to, he examined my water and discovered I had a little sugar in my water. He straight away phoned a specialist in Harley Street, and I went there for an examination.

They looked me all over, particularly my heart, which was alright. The diagnosis was Diabetes. It meant I had to take a little pill every day to see if I could regulate it. I was shocked by the result. I shouldn't have that complaint. I seemed so fit, did a lot of sport. I soon got used to it, and hopefully, I could keep it controlled. I had to go to Romford once a year to see the top man.

One evening on Wednesday, I always had to work late that night. There was a knock on my window facing the front garden. There was a lady standing there, an old lady who asked me if I had lost my Alsatian. I told her I had not had a dog for about a year. She said she had a lovely dog in her kitchen, as she had her own dog in the house. It had been with her since early evening. She didn't know what to do with it. I said to Fay go and have a look. I had missed Sabre all the time I was without her. So, Fay went with the lady to her house and stayed for about an hour. She finally came back and said, what a lovely dog it was. You must see this dog, he is lovely. We went back with some string and brought him home. It was now nearly 23.45 pm. I took him for a walk towards the golf course. We kept him after that and reported it to the police as the actual owner might be looking for him.

He was approximately a year old, we think, and we named him Prince. It wasn't very long before he had his first fight, which he lost.

A chow stood at the entrance of the park, Prince, who was in the park not on the lead, went to play with it, and the chow turned around and bit him. A few weeks later, we went to the park at night with him. A dog in the back garden of someone's house got hold of him by the neck and would not let go. It took me all my strength to get the dog off Prince, who then changed. The next time he was in the park, if a dog came by, Prince would approach, bitches didn't bother him, but if they were male, Prince wanted to bite and fight. This became difficult as he loved to be free from the lead. I used to take him to the park early in the morning at 07:00 am before anybody was about so that he could be free.

Marilyn had her first boy Richard in 1977 and the second, Stuart, in 1980. Then we had more trouble with Prince. He had been good until one evening in March we went for a walk. We heard people in the bushes opposite the park. Prince went inside the bushes and chased a dog out. He caught and got hold of it by the park gates. I fell over on the road trying to separate the two dogs but eventually succeeded. Then it happened. It was Fay's 50th birthday on the 28th of March. In the afternoon, she wanted to take Prince for a walk in the park. As she opened the back door, a man walked past with his dog, who had a bandage over his ear. It was the dog Prince attacked the other night.

Fay realising it was that dog said to the man, "you go to the park, and I'll follow shortly". She did but perhaps too soon, and when she got in the park, the other dog was ahead, perhaps about 50 yards. Prince saw him and started to pull. Fay pulled him by the choke chain. Prince turned around and nipped her in the thigh. That was it. She didn't want to keep him anymore. She had lost faith and said he must go. We offered him to the police, but they could not take him as we had no papers about his pedigree. She then phoned the RAF; they came down, took him to the park, tested his reactions to gunshots, and took him away in a van. I never saw him again. We were sent some pictures of him, one with his RAF trainer and handler and one with the young lady who groomed him. He looked beautiful.

We became a limited company with Geoffrey, a Director, and Fay, a Director and Secretary. Geoffrey and Marilyn had their third child, another boy named Scott. Fay would like them to have had a little girl. It wasn't to be. Time went by, and in 1981 Fay and I went for a holiday in Israel. One morning we went for a walk. We passed a young lady with pamphlets regarding timeshare. She gave us one. It was a lovely hotel on the beach about 15 minutes from Tel-Aviv. We told her we might be interested, so she took us to the office. They gave us coffee, ordered a taxi, and drove us to the hotel, which was in an advanced state of completion. We saw the show flat, liked it and said we would consider it. The show flat was on the 7th floor, with a very nice east-facing view catching the sun from first thing in the morning till late afternoon. Two days later we bought two weeks in the show flat. The hotel was not ready till 1982, but I returned for the opening. It was lovely.

When I arrived at my sister's flat in Israel, where I stayed, my brother-in-law told me that England was at war. I said, "you must be joking", but it was true. The Falklands had been invaded.

The first year of the timeshare was fantastic. It soon changed. There were not enough people coming to the hotel. We used it for six years, including two holidays in the States. In September 1985, we were going to our timeshare in Israel, and on our departure day, we had been to the warehouse, as usual, went home a little early as we were going to Heathrow by train. We had prepared the night before our cases and the food to take with us. Tins of salmon and other things are less available in Israel. Fay said I have some matzo meal, a fine type of flour, and will take that. When we got to Heathrow, we were going by British Airways. We got to the security. Fay was with one guy, and I got a young man. He opens the case and finds the matzo meal. It looked like flour; it could be cocaine, so he asked me what it was. I shouted over to Fay, what is that and as she explained, I told the chap that this is to bind the salmon when making cutlets. I said you make round things with these, move them from hand to hand, rub them in the matzo meal, put them in the frying pan, and they come out brown. Can you imagine the laughter from all the other passengers who were nearby? The fellow saw the joke and let us go; perhaps he should have examined the white stuff. However, it gave us a good laugh.

Darren had his 13th birthday party in 1987, and we took him with us to the States to Orlando for three weeks. Eventually, our timeshare folded. A great pity, we just about covered our expenses over the holiday period we enjoyed. In about the middle of August that year, we went to my sister-in-law for tea and supper. We had fried fish which I shouldn't have had. In the night, I became very sick. It felt as though the walls were moving towards me. I got up that morning feeling awfully giddy. I couldn't go to work that day, something I had never done before in the last 30 years. I went to see the specialist at Romford, had my sugar tested, and was told I wasn't well and should have to use insulin for the rest of my life. I was devastated. Later the following month, I started using it and have been fine ever since.

28th August 1988. Tomorrow is the 40th anniversary of the London Korfball Association, of which I was a former member and chairman. They arranged a big tournament to be played in the summer on the 29th of August. I was invited to play in an old England team, and I, of course, accepted.

Meanwhile, we had put our bungalow up for sale. We arranged for a new estate agent to look at the property. He liked what he saw and said, "I'll sell that for you". The next morning on Sunday, we had a phone call from a man, a bachelor, to view the property. After his viewing, he straight away decided to buy it. We started to look around to buy a property to move onto. I'd always hoped for something by the seaside, where I wanted eventually to retire. We found a lovely block of flats on the front called The Overcliff. The flat we were interested in was on the 7th floor, overlooking the sea from all rooms and impressive.

We agreed on a price with the vendor and the time involved. Anyway, in the end, he gazumped us and sold it over our head to someone else. So, we had to make a hasty decision to buy somewhere else in a hurry as we had that buyer for the bungalow. I came to Westcliff again and looked at some flats about 500 yards away from the other one. It was much cheaper, lovely view except there was no lift at my age and soon that could be a problem. However, we bought it in the hope to get back to the block of flats just up the road which we had just lost.

We moved and were quite happy still going to London to work, and it wasn't very long, about eight months we got a letter from the estate agent here in town that the flat next door to the one we lost was available. It was an even more beautiful flat as it was all on the front. They wanted an awful lot of money, so we made an offer. They did not answer. So, another month went by, and they dropped the price below what we offered. We then took the plunge. We bought it, but we had to put our flat up for sale. I then committed the most horrible thing I did in my life. I took a bridging loan for £75,000. I must have been mad, but I wanted the flat, and a front-facing one might not become available for a long time.

We put our flat up for sale, and after a few weeks, a young man came along, another bachelor, he saw it on a Saturday morning liked what he saw and realising that he had not to spend any money on it, said he would like to buy it. He saw the garage also, and then I directed him back to the estate agent, where he placed his deposit. My bridging loan was only for five weeks, a thing one never hopes to have to do. It could have been many months. At the beginning of May, we moved and had been at the other flat for exactly one year.

Today is Saturday, and tomorrow is the big tournament. It's also our 40th wedding anniversary. I have booked a hotel in Reigate Surrey where Fay and I will have dinner, and a dance, stay the night and be not far away from the big tournament tomorrow. I arrived at the ground very fresh on Sunday for the games. One of my players who played in the first international against Holland in 1948, Vera Engels, was also there. We had a fair team but did not play in the top section. We played well and won the cup, which was presented to Vera and me at the same time. In one of the matches, I scored a lovely goal from a long way out, and Fay took a picture just before the ball entered the basket. A nice souvenir.

I am 63 years of age, and in England, nobody would play in that age group.

We had been living at the Overcliff now for about two years. It is time I started to think about retiring from work. I have just looked at a car which I hope to purchase. It belongs to the Managing Director of the Rover company. It is an almost new Rover 827 SLI. Done 3,376 miles in nine months and is top of the range. The color is racing green, very beautiful. It really has only just been run in. Deciding to buy the car. I am delighted with it. I hope to use it for many years.

We have put the business up for sale, and a gentleman is very interested. He would like to have a lease on the property and take over all the customers. We agreed, and so I'll retire at the end of August. Geoffrey, who is now 39, is also leaving the business; however, Harvey is staying on with the new owner. Hopefully, it will work out.

It is now September, and I have stopped working. Fay and I will go to France in the car and visit my friends in Dordogne, from there we will go to Cannes for a couple of weeks. One day while we were in Dordogne, we met an Englishman in a small town and started talking. He was a pilot during the war. I told him I was an air gunner and asked him where he lived. He told me Morpeth in Northumberland. What a coincidence. I got my wings up there as I was there with 14 other Dutch lads to learn to become air gunners. He said, "were you there in 1943", I said "yes", because there was an article in the local paper only two weeks ago where a Dutchman, age 73, went to Morpeth to try to find the grave of his brother-in-law, who had died in that crash.

This man promised me a cutting of the article when he returned to England. I did not wait for his paper so when I got back, I phoned the operator of the telephone service, she said she could not help me find the address of a newspaper without a name, but I could try a company in Avon called Telephones. The guy at the other end was very friendly, and within two minutes, I had three names of papers in Morpeth. The first one was the Herald and Post, so I decided to try them first. I was told the editor was busy but would phone me back. Within half an hour, I had a phone call, and the lady

editor was pleased to hear from me. She understood from the original article that the Dutchman had not found the grave. I told her there could not be a lot of cemeteries in Morpeth and start from there, to phone the churches. She soon came back to me with the cemeteries name, the grave number and the name of the lad who was buried there with all the others. He was one of my 3 other roommates, two of which had been in the crash.

Another half-hour went by, and the editor returned to me and said she had the address of the Dutch person who came over. I promised to write to him in Dutch. I did straight away. Within a fortnight, I had a phone call on a Saturday evening from this man, Mr Velleman of Terneuzen. He was delighted to hear from me, the reason he had come to England was the fact that his wife is very ill mentally, lost her brother all these years ago in England, had lost another brother some years ago to suicide and since she lost her mother a couple of years ago, became mentally ill, the man himself is 73 and suffering from cancer. We are going to keep in touch with each other.

As I had time on my hands, I started to think about other things, such as what happened to my friend, another air gunner, who retired after the war to Canada. I really mean emigrated. I had an address in my little book and looked it up, but there was no phone number. I decided to write to the town hall of the place where we originally went. It was Georgetown, Ontario. I sent a letter there, and within 3 weeks, I got an answer from them to tell me that this person was still registered with them for tax, gave me their new address and phone number, mentioned that they tried the number but got no answer wished me a Happy New Year. I phoned the given number 4 times that weekend, even at 05:00 am, as I realised that they were hours behind us over there.

The same evening Saturday at 20:00 pm, there was a phone call from Tampa in the United States of America. It was my friend Maurice; he had received a letter from his town hall, and we spoke for about 15 minutes. It was great after 46 years. Hopefully, we may meet in 1992. The reason he was in Tampa, he explained, was that the weather in Canada in winter is very cold, and so he said he and his wife have an apartment in Tampa where they go from November till early April. So that is a little success.

One night there was a program on television called Witness to Survival, and it told the story of two air gunners who survived a crash in France during a bombing raid in 1943. I watched the film of that event and wondered, if still alive, what happened to the four airmen we found off the Dutch coat way back in July 1943. Maybe they all perished soon afterwards in another raid after the usual leave. If any are still alive, it would be nice if we met for the first time after all these years, either here or in the States, and so I have written to this program as they asked for interesting stories. Up to now, I have not heard, but I am hopeful.

I am now retired some six months and play snooker about four times a week, swim twice a week, play tennis at the weekend and play cards Monday afternoons. Fay and I have been going tea dancing at the Cliffs Pavilion, which is just around the corner. A couple of weeks ago we went to Paris by coach for six days and enjoyed ourselves. Next week it's Fay's birthday, and we'll be going to Brussels for four days, visit Antwerp and go to my father's grave, just over the border in Putte, Holland. My grandson Darren is 18 today, and last Saturday, we had a birthday party in a wine bar in Barking, Essex for him, and there were over two hundred friends. It was a great success.

Yesterday we went for a ride to Woking in Surrey to visit my friends Air Gunners grave. Jimmy the chap who almost died when he came back from a bombing trip to France in 1944. I felt very emotional but so pleased I went. The cemetery was for War Graves, Americans, Canadians, Polish, Dutch and all European nationals. I took a lot of photographs.

A few more weeks and it will be the 10th of May. That will be the end of my experience and the time it has taken to write this book. A life's journey beginning 10th May 1940 until now, spanning what happened over 52 years, half a lifetime. Whoever reads this might find it most interesting, I hope.

Sal, Fre his sister and Sophie his mother

Fre, Uncle Max & Auntie Toe Chobitz

Sal in uniform

Sal and friend in naval uniform

Sal in uniform

Fre and Sophie

Fay and Sal Wedding day

Left to Right

Davey-Alf-Shirley-Annie-Sophie-Fray-Sal-Sandra-Jaap-Fay-Ivon-Yopie-
Booba-Bernard-Kitty-Alec-Anne-Hymie-Ray

Sal at korfball match in London

Geoffrey and Hilary

Family Portrait

Sal - Hilary - Geoff - Fay

Fay and Sal

Sal as head match day official, international Holland vs Belgium

Sal in full Korfball referee attire.

BEC Korfball Club, Spot Sal second on from the left at the back

(Papa mentions Loughborough hotel dancing in the diary httpsi1.wp.comwww.brixtonbuzz.comwp-contentuploads201304loughborough-hotel-pub-05.jpg)

(I found this pic on the wartime memories project 320 squadrons. In the original photo, there was a caption underneath naming all these young men, including your Sal, top row 3rd from left. 5 of these men died on 29/3/1943 in an air training accident

Aircrew Remembered Aviation Personal Histories and Databases)

SAL'S DIARY

Friday 10th May 1940

Starts with the raid of Germany in the Netherlands. The same night round morning, Germany committed violations of neutrality in Belgium. They come over with 38 and 50 at the same time and throw firebombs and others. It takes about 4 hours. It means Germany have started a war with Belgium. During the night attacks by aeroplanes and fighting in the air.

Saturday 11th May 1940

Attacks are going on. Sleepless nights.

Sunday 12th May 1940

Still the same scenes. In the evening, a statement that boys and men between the ages of 16 and 35 years must leave the country and must depart to Roeselare. Me, although not yet 16, departed too because if the Germans occupied Antwerp, I had to work for them.

Monday 13th May 1940

I went by bicycle to Roeselare. Before I went, there was an enormous nervous sense in our house. I was emotional. I left and came with a group of eight young men, all of them from Deurne. Our captain was Louis from the swimming pool (the little captain). In the late afternoon, we arrived in Roeselare. It was chaos. They didn't expect us so soon. We found shelter to sleep...

Tuesday 14th May 1940

In the late afternoon, we departed to Ieperen. When we arrived, it was the same chaos as in Roeselare. They allowed us to go further to Poperinge. At Poperinge, evacuees were allowed to drive to France. We drove on to a little place before France called Abeele. There we again found shelter to sleep because the border was closed. We would wait until the next day...

Wednesday 15th May 1940

We cycled to the border. We were all okay except one, and that was me. I had to be left alone because I was an Englishman. The others drove through and told me we would meet in Gasselt. After musing for about an hour, I saw an old acquaintance coming, Max Pels. We met and were, in a short time, good friends. He was with two other friends. At 11.00 am, we were allowed to pass the border. We left for Gasselt, but there was nothing there, so we moved on to another little place called Ochtezeele. It was the third day that we got some food. One loaf of bread per 10 men.

Thursday 16th May 1940

We cycled to Rubrouck. We stayed there just for the day in the refugee camp. It was so bad that we left two boys there and ran away together with four young men around 30 years old by late in the afternoon. About 20 km from Boulogne. A car came towards us in the distance, and when he drove close, I raised my hand, and he stopped at the top of the mountain. We hitchhiked and arrived that same evening in Boulogne. We found a little shed and slept there amongst the dust of potatoes.

Friday 17th May 1940

We stayed in the city. We heard that a train was leaving for Paris at 12.00 in the afternoon. We went to the house, packed our belongings and left. Two of the six men stayed there. We cycled to the station and saw Bill Bouteille. He asked us where we were going, and we told him that we wanted to head for Paris. He told us that we should try to go to Le Havre and from there cross the Channel to England. He promised a job in the diamond trade. We got our tickets from the office to Le Havre, passing through Amiens. The other two men got their tickets to Paris. Bill had the people of Preso, the married son Willie and his wife with him. So, we left Boulogne and arrived the next day in Amiens. The Germans had bombarded Amiens that very night.

Saturday 18th of May 1940

Arriving in Amiens, we thought we could get a link to Le Havre. But everything there was chaos, and there was no link. We packed our luggage, and, on our bicycles, we left the station and went on the road to Rouen. About 30km before Amiens, there was a little place, Poix. We could take there a train to Rouen. When we got to Poix, we stayed at the station until the express train to Le Havre came. At 11.00 we arrived in Le Havre, in the middle of the bombs. Daar Op Het station was a Red Cross position, and we were offered a meal for free. Mothers came there with their children, some of them in their nightgowns. There was even a woman with a baby of eight days old, and although she was not allowed to go on the streets, she did anyway to have her baby baptized by a priest.

Wednesday 22nd May 1940

I stayed in Le Havre for a few days. Each day I visited the British Consulate to obtain a passport. On the first day, I saw there Mr Kloot and went to him immediately. He told me his wife was downstairs with Hanneke. Mr and Mrs Gobits were also there with Jupie. They also were trying to get their passports. I received my passport the same day. A ship was meant to depart on 20th May, but the Germans had placed mines so that the ship couldn't enter or leave port. It was then, on 22nd May, the consulate announced that only British nationals could come to England. A ship was to be boarded at 14:00 pm, but by 19:00 pm, the ship had only just arrived. We left port at 20:00 pm. Max Pels went that same day with his friend Bill to Bordeaux. He gave me his last money for my trip to England. The families Kloot and Gobits left for the South.

Thursday 23rd May 1940

Arrival in Southampton. My papers had to be checked, and with everything being okay, a train was ready and waiting, destination London. I should also say when back in Le Havre, I met a priest in the consulate. I had no money for the boat, and he offered to give me 10 /. I refused and told him that I didn't need it now. On reaching

Southampton, I changed my French money. I had 85 Francs and received 9/4 in exchange.

When we arrived in London, we were transferred to a camp. It was a children's hospital. There were other refugees, most of the people were Polish, and between them, I saw the Dutch group of Wijnschenk. We stayed there for four days. In fact, I, with the people of Wijnschenk, were moved on earlier than otherwise. It might have been because they had already spent a week at the camp.

Sunday 26th May 1940

Today South Norwood, I was placed in one of the richest hotels in that neighbourhood, The Beaulieu Heights Hotel. Such a delicious variety of food, I never had such splendour in my family before. I stayed there four days and was transferred then to Brixton, the reason being the hotel was too expensive.

Thursday 30th May 1940

So I was transferred again. At my new house were six men from Turnhout Belgium and a seventh boy my age who only spoke French. I had to speak three languages at the same time. We immediately became good friends, and on the first evening, most of us played billiards.

Sunday 2nd June 1940

I went with Emile Delvigne to the amusements. I lost 2/6[12p]. That same afternoon I met Rose Ford.

Sunday 9th June 1940

I went to the Labour Exchange. They sent me to the Employment Exchange, and I was told to be back in the morning.

Monday 10th June 1940

Arriving at the Employment Exchange early. I made a telephone call to the office of Geo Monro. They wanted to meet me, so I went, and they hired me immediately. I ended with Rose, and I met with Florrie that same evening.

Tuesday 11th June 1940

First day of my job. I was out of bed an hour early. The work was not too bad.

Wednesday 12th June 1940

I am in the elevator, and I meet Joan. She asked me if I liked it here. I say yes. On the second floor, I go out of the elevator first because I thought she was the lift girl. But she also came out of the elevator. Rather embarrassed, I asked the boy who teaches me to go to Joan to offer my excuses. The same day we were already good friends.

Saturday 15th June 1940

I ended with Florrie.

Monday 17th June 1940

I met Irene. We went to the park, and she gave me an arm. That same evening it was already done.

Saturday 22nd June 1940

I met Nancy. She is a new girlfriend for me. Before I go home, I give her a kiss.

Sunday 23rd June 1940

Irene is making a fault for the first time. She should come at 08:00 am. She arrives at 09:30 am. I was very angry.

Monday 24th June 1940

Irene is telling me she loves me but also someone else. I'd really like to finish with her, so tell her I want to talk with my friends. I don't shake hands with her, nothing. She says it was a joke, but I don't like those kinds of jokes. I'm not too bothered because there are enough girls here to get. They love, most of all, strangers and soldiers. I will not disapprove of them.

Thursday 27th June 1940

I was taking my letters and delivering just one of them at Marks & Spencer when I saw in a side street people standing there. One of them looked very much like a girl from the Barber family. I went back again, and then I saw Mr Barber standing there, and I went to greet him. The Sluis family was also with them. We talked for a while and then Mrs Barber told me to go to The Foresters, maybe they could do something for me. I went that same afternoon, but the person I needed had just left for the day.

Friday 28th June 1940

I tried the Foresters again. This time I managed to talk to the person, and he told me I couldn't get anything because I was not a member yet. So, I left again. They look like animals.

Saturday 29th June 1940

This was a real peach. I left home by bicycle at 07.30 am. I was halfway when my bicycle chain came off, and I couldn't get it back on the bike again. I had to walk for quite a long time. I was 20 minutes late for work. On my way home after work, I had managed to fix my bicycle chain. I was biking for five minutes and got a puncture. I had to walk again and came home dead tired.

That same evening my friend Mr Delvinge came home drunk. I was afraid to sleep next to him.

Sunday 30th June 1940

We, Emile and I, went to the park and followed there three girls. My heart immediately started racing. When I could get one of the three, I immediately finished with Irene.

Monday 1st July 1940

I've been to Eaton Square. I've got some clothes, a costume, a pair of shoes, pyjamas, two pairs of socks, a shirt and underpants, and a shirt there. I come home at 17:00 pm, try my outfit again, and everyone starts laughing. The outfit is too big for me. One of the men tried the clothes, which was exactly his size. He bought them from me for 15 [75p]/. For that money, I can now purchase long grey trousers, wear my blue cardigan with them and am ready for the whole summer. If I save more money from my allowance, come winter, I can buy a winter outfit.

In the evening I went to the park, but Irene was not there. So, I finished with her. So, it is three girls in four weeks, not too bad. I can get other girls, but they are not my cup of tea. That same evening Emile came home drunk again. This time not as drunk as last time, but drunk is drunk.

Tuesday 2nd July 1940

I met a few new people. They are the people who have the people of Vilvoorde in their house. They have a lovely daughter; I mean the people of the house, not Vilvoorde. She will do that.

Wednesday 3rd July 1940

When I'm helping Joan late in the afternoon with calculating, Miss Webber, an old woman from our department, comes in, and she looks at me. She will tell me today, and it's not good news. What a dirty thing of Miss Webber. She is not talking but starts yelling.

Thursday 4th July 1940

We, Emile and myself, went again to the park and again had a lot of attention. For the first time, I wore my new trousers, which made me look taller.

Yesterday Miss Webber washed her hands, and when she came back, she came to me. She started talking about my mother and sister and asked if I had heard something from them. She felt that she had played a dirty role, and she had remorse.

Friday 5th July 1940

Irene came to the park and sat with the people of Vilvoorde. I hardly spoke to her.

Saturday 6th July 1940

She came again and asked me if I wanted to walk with her. On our way home, she said she knew that I was done with her, but she wasn't done with me. So that evening it got good again.

Monday 8th July 1940

She came to my work, and we went for a walk. Now she is coming every day.

Tuesday 9th July 1940

I had been to her work. It's five minutes from mine. She is working in the Great Queen Street. I'm on the King Street. I write this because Queen means in Dutch Koningin and King means Koning.

Wednesday 10th July 1940

I had been to the park in the pouring rain. First, I had been to 99 Bunhill Row for my cousin, Emanuel Verduin, but the only thing there was a desk. That same evening, I got new friends. From one of them, Ernie, I have got a hat. And it makes me look very good. There is also an Italian boy but a British national by birth. I told him about my job, and he immediately wanted to ask his boss if he could use me the next day. He said I could earn maybe 24/[£1.20p], but I asked him to wait a little while. That evening the boys brought me home.

Thursday 11th July 1940

I made a telephone call to Bunhill Row. They told me he wasn't there anymore and gave me his address. I was surprised it was so far away from London. It's in Clifton.

Friday 12th July 1940

Again I finished with Irene. Again, she is not coming.

Saturday 13th July 1940

I count all the girls I can get and figure it out that at this moment, I can get seven girls for sure. I don't mention the ones who are not sure. Isn't it terrible?

Sunday 14th July 1940

I wrote a letter to my cousin and hoped that I would have an answer soon.

Tuesday 16th of July 1940

It is unbelievable, but I got homesick for the first time. Because of that, I feel very ill. Really ill and homesick, as the English say. I told my friends I was a naughty boy, and because of that, I got homesick. They talked about penance. I think I've had suffered enough for a long time without penance. I believe that if the refugees go back, I will do the same.

Friday 19th July 1940

For the first time, I went swimming. That same evening I've received the hat from Ernie. It suits me.

Monday 22nd July 1940

In the evening, I have been to Woolworth to buy a bag for a gas mask. They didn't have it, so I went back and bumped into a man saying pardon me, in Flemish. I went back to him and said, "Hi, are you guys from Belgium?" And they said yes. They also came from Antwerp, even from Deurne-South. They lived on the Boterlaer Baan. So, 5 minutes away from where we lived. I told them to come to the park. They asked me if I knew their daughter. She went to school in Eyke street. Her name is Mariëtte. I will meet her in the coming days.

That evening I went to the park. Lily asked me to go for a walk. I went with her but didn't have any idea that something else was behind it... When we came back, I had to sleep on her lap.

When I went home, I said goodbye to Lily and Winnie, a man came walking next to me and started talking. He said at once that he wasn't married and knew just a few women, but that some of them he took to his room. He rubbed his hand all the time over my pocket. Fortunately, my wallet was in my other pocket. Then he grabbed my thumb and started to play with it. I do mean my thumb; in England, it means something else. If he had done that, I would have given him a sledgehammer blow in his face and ran away.

Tuesday 23rd July 1940

This morning, they took away my towel again, for the whole day, I hated that. I went this afternoon to buy cookies, and when I came back, my cousin Emanuel was in the office. Of course, I was surprised. He had no time, unfortunately. Otherwise, he would have stayed longer than he did. When he left, he gave me 2/ [10p]. He also spoke with Mr Towler, my boss. He said he was very satisfied with me. Cousin Emanuel comes back to London in a few weeks. I hope that he will have more time then to talk with me. When he was gone, I went to Mr Oldsworth and spoke with him about Cousin Emanuel. Mr Oldsworth said that he would talk with Cousin Emanuel if he came to visit me again. I hope that then he will have success.

Saturday 27th July 1940

Today I've got 2/ [10p] from a man who sells downstairs to go out. I didn't want to accept it, but other people told me to take it. He could easily miss it. So, I put the money in my clothes.

Sunday 28th July 1940

I went to the park and listened again to the music there. It was the best band that we had heard in six weeks. I also saw the people of Brussels with the woman of Paris. Again, I walked with them.

Monday 29th July 1940

Yesterday evening I have been to Camberwell. There was an evening for the refugees from Belgium, Holland, France and some English people who were glad to come. I had a great laugh there. I met a boy from Antwerp and Bruges. Also, I met two Dutch girls from The Hague. We talked to a young priest from Amsterdam who had lived in Belgium for a long time. He had been in the Belgian Congo for the past three years. He had walked from Luik to Calais. There was also a complicated soldier there. He wore an English outfit with the French colours on his breast, but he was Belgian.

Tuesday 30th July 1940

The second week of the holiday, my friend Mr Stokes has come. I miss him very much. With him, I can talk about whatever I want. Every day I gave him 2 pence. So, at the end of the week, it was 1/ [5p]. That money I could put towards my clothes.

Friday 2nd August 1940

I have been with Mr Seville to the cinema. He's the man who is living with us in our house. It's the first time I went out. I've seen Souls at Sea (Zeeschuimers) starring George Raft, Gary Cooper and Francis Dee. The second movie was Waikiki Wedding with Bing Crosby, Shirley Ross and Bob Burns.

Saturday 3rd August 1940

One of the most important days for my wallet. I didn't spend any money that day. It's really a miracle.

Sunday 4th August 1940

I went to the park and met two new girls. Their names were Gladys and Zena.

Monday 5th August 1940

Again we have been to Camberwell to go out dancing. I made a new love there. We talked to English girls and danced with them. One of them spoke for her girlfriend. She asked me if I could come Sunday to dance. I have been waltzing with Emile. It was perfect, but when he should have let me go, I fell down to the ground.

At 22.30, it came to an end, and we wanted to bring the girl back home, but her father waited outside for her, and they even got into a fight because she was five minutes late.

Tuesday 6th August 1940

Today Mr Stokes came back from his holiday. Yesterday we worked overtime for one hour and 15 minutes because Monday we had a day off. That is 4 times a year. Yesterday evening I went to a tea evening for the refugees at Solon road. Of course, it was nothing. There were five English girls and one Belgian. Later, when all the Belgian people were gone, we were introduced to the English girls, and again we had new girlfriends. Now I hardly can count them anymore. Later at 8 o'clock, I went to Kensington Park and talked with Gladys and Zena, and I had to read English to them. It wasn't easy at all, but I made just a few mistakes.

Wednesday 7th August 1940

This morning I spoke with three French sailors. It must have been for five minutes. Hardly 10 minutes later, I see the first Belgian car in London. It was from a doctor.

Thursday 8th August 1940

Late in the afternoon, when I came back home, along with the Red Cross, I wrote to Mum and Fre. I hope that the telegram will arrive. Are they alright and still at home? I can expect an answer in a week or five or six.

Sunday 11th August 1940

Late in the afternoon, when I brought my letters to Mr Oldsworth, I talked with him about my salary. I asked him for a raise. He should see what he could do for me. The same evening, I went to Camberwell for dancing. The girl from that Monday was already waiting there. When I saw her up close, I was shocked that I had given her away as a girlfriend. She had brought a friend; her name was Vera. With this girl, I have danced five times. I also got her back home.

Monday 12th August 1940

Again I went to Camberwell for dancing. It was again the regular evening for refugees. That evening I brought Vera back home again. That evening the other girl fought with Vera because Vera had taken me away from her.

Tuesday 13th August 1940

Went again in the evening to Solon road. It's later in the afternoon. There I talked to the people of Deurne-South. They were there with their daughter. Of course, I knew her already, I mean her face.

Wednesday 15th August 1940

I've been listening to music with Irene. I met someone I know from my work and asked him to stay with us. He agreed and was delighted about Irene. From that time on, we remained best friends, and still, we are.

Thursday 16th August 1940

In the morning, George and Charlie both offered me money. George wanted to give me 5/ [25p] for myself and my clothes, and Charlie offered me 2/6d. [12p] I didn't want to accept it because they are workmen who have women and children. At 5 o'clock they showed me their wages. It was £5. 7. 9. [£5.40p] (in normal times in our currency 645,50 Francs). Of course, don't forget that life in England is more expensive than in Belgium.

At 12.30 in the afternoon, the sirens have blared. We have been sitting in the air-raid shelter for one hour.

At 4 o'clock when we received our money, my salary was still the same. Of course, I hated it. I had hoped for that the whole week. My boss told me to go downstairs again.

Saturday 17th August 1940

In the afternoon I did some shopping for myself with Madame Williams. We bought trousers, and the price was 6/6. [32p] I had given only 5/ [25p] to madame for my trousers. She also bought me two underpants and a nice shirt. Altogether, I mean also the 1/6

[8p]more for my trousers she has spent 8/5d [42p]. I told her that if I got my raised salary, I would give her the money back as soon as possible. But she didn't want to hear it.

Sunday 18th August 1940

Again went dancing. The father of one of the girls, Cathleen, saw me and told her that I should come to him Monday evening so that we could speak with each other. That same evening, I wanted to fight, but the boy with whom I wanted to fight didn't want to.

There was a slow waltz. I stood up and asked Vera for this dance. A boy was with her already the whole evening, but now I asked her. I stood up, and she stood up. Suddenly the boy grabbed her and wanted to dance with her. I said, " I asked her first", and he replied, "I'll take her", so I said, "Then I'll take you outside, and we are going to fight". He didn't want that, so he left the girl for me. In the late afternoon, there were air-raid sirens. The planes hovered above our district for more than 55 minutes.

Monday 19th August 1940

Today is Fre's birthday. She turned 18 years old. I'm hoping she is enjoying her birthday. In the afternoon, I went to drink tea with

George. In the evening Harry went with me to dance. Before we went, he took Edward and me to a cafe where I had my first glass of beer. Harry is a very good dancer. There were girls there who could dance, but even they couldn't follow him.

Cathleen asked her friend if she would ask me which of the girls I should take, Cathleen or Vera. I answered none of them. That was the best answer I could have given.

Within myself, I wish all the best for my beloved sister and mother.

Tuesday 20th August 1940

I went with Con, the cashier, to the library and found there on his membership a nice book. It's called 'The Dance for the Gallows'.

Wednesday 21st August 1940

In the afternoon, I went with Harry to a cafe, and we had a cup of tea. In the evening, I visited him and began to teach him some basic Dutch language. We bought books ready for his first lesson. It went well. I saw his wife there. Harry never told me he was married. By 22:00 pm, I was eating lovely fresh bread with good butter and salmon. It was a wonderful evening.

Friday 23rd August 1940

This morning at 04:00 am, we had an air-raid alarm again. This afternoon I've got my salary. I thought maybe I would have my 2/6 [12p] raise, but it was no good. Instead, it was half as much, just 5 / [25p]. Now I've earned 150 francs if I count it from before the war. An excellent salary for a boy of 15. Also, it is a fantastic salary because I'm two months working at the office and three months in England.

Saturday 24th August 1940

This morning at 08.30 am, again, an air-raid alarm went off. I offered myself as a messenger of the air defence on our work if it is necessary. Today there came two guests, the daughter of Mr Seville and her friend. The daughter is 28 and looks so ugly. Her friend is 33, and she looks okay.

Sunday 25th August 1940

I've slept until 13:00 pm. That was because of the air-raid alarm. In the evening I went dancing. Harry and his wife came as well. I danced with his wife a waltz, and she taught me very well. In the second dance, a girl came for me. That was something! I've had an amusing evening. There was an air-raid alarm during dance time. When I came home wanting to sleep, there came another.

Monday 26th August 1940

Again I have been to Camberwell and met two new girls and a friend. That evening there was an alarm that took six hours. I stayed in Camberwell until 03:30 am. I finally arrived home and was back in my bed by 04:00 am. At 07:00 am, I couldn't get out of my bed. I ended up arriving at work eighteen minutes late because I had overslept.

Tuesday 27th August 1940

Again there were two air-raid alarms. The guests are not having a nice time on their holiday. They had to come to London and go out every day.

Wednesday 28th August 1940

Again an air-raid alarm, 20:30 pm. This alarm took 7 hours, so it was a new record. I was outside with one of the guests, and it was dark. It was the friend of Mr Saville's daughter. She stayed with me the whole time. Sometimes she took her arm around me, or she did another crazy thing, if that was possible. Later that evening, she asked me to kiss her. I did it with pleasure. The difference between 15 and 33 is a nice number. For me, it is a new record. I will go on with her till Sunday. So, it is just four days. Anyway, I will see to taking advantage of it.

Saturday 31st August 1940

On this day, we had the air-raid alarms six times. In the late afternoon, I was sleeping, and when I woke up, there was an alarm again.

That night I've seen the shooting down of three aeroplanes. It could have been either English or German aeroplanes. In the morning, when I brought down the books, I've got from Mr Goley 1/ [5p] again and from Mr Wilson 2/6. [12p] That's great. In the morning, a policeman came to our house for information about my nationality.

He told Mrs Williams that he would call me another time. Until now, I didn't hear anything about it.

Sunday 1st September 1940

Today we only had two air-raid alarms. The girls have left already. They took pictures of us and one picture of me with that one guest.

Monday 2nd September 1940

Again there was an air-raid alarm. Happily, not too long.

Tuesday 3rd September 1940

Three air-raid alarms. That's all.

Wednesday 4th September 1940

It was 13:30 pm, and just now, the second air-raid alarm went off. It's precisely my lunchtime. I mean one-hour mealtime. Coincidentally I'm not going out, because I must keep my diary. If I go downstairs now, I have some music again. Because there are two people who play on the piano in the bomb shelter when there is an air-raid alarm. Today we had another alarm after this one, which brings the number to three.

Thursday 5th September 1940

Yesterday we had three alarms again.

Friday 6th September 1940

Again air-raid alarms.

Saturday 7th September 1940

The air offensive started. A lot of bombs were thrown, and many people were killed. Four hundred were killed, and one thousand four hundred were injured. Big fires broke out at the docks.

Sunday 8th September 1940

Again it was a terrible night. The alarm lasted from 20:00 pm until 06:30 am. A lot of bombs were thrown again and very close by again. I through myself to the ground several times. I just slept for just one hour. I think that tonight when it starts again, I will go to a bomb shelter and wait there for the things to come.

Monday 9th September 1940

I came home from work at 16:30 pm, and at 17:00 pm, the sirens went off. It continued until 19:15 pm. I've seen many German planes. Later in the evening, at 20:30, there was an air-raid alarm again. Emile came home and told me to come with him to the bomb shelter. We took our blankets and walked quickly to the hideout.

We stayed for nine hours in the bomb shelter. By the time we arrived back home, it was at 06:00 am. We had to make a detour because of a time bomb that had fallen not far away from us. We saw Mr Saville in the garden. He beckoned us. I thought he was angry because I was in the bomb shelter. But it was something quite different. In the garden next to us there had been fallen another bomb.

Three meters from where his bomb shelter was, there were people inside. Nobody was killed or hurt.

The chicken coop was gone with all the chickens who were in there. Rocks and stone had fallen in our garden, and we found pieces of the bomb. Further on in the street, another bomb dropped. The damage was more significant there. Many of the windows had been broken. It was incredible luck that nobody was hurt.

Close to the house where a man was sleeping, a massive stone had fallen with just one of the windows being broken in their room. He was okay.

I may say that at this moment it is terrible in London. Today I received a letter from my cousin Emanuel, and he asked me if I could give him my sizes because he had some clothes that could be good for me. I will answer him the day after tomorrow. He also has a sweater that his wife knitted for me at home.

Tuesday 10th September 1940

We have had five air-raid alarms. One was at 12:30 am, one at 04:00 am, one at 05:00 am, one at 06:00 am, and the last one at 08:15

am. This time I did fall asleep because I was dead tired. So, I slept between the bombs and came good out of it.

Wednesday 11th September 1940

Harry didn't come to work yesterday. I wanted to see him; I was worried if his house had been bombed. I could not go, there were no streetcars, so I planned to go this evening.

I spoke with his father, who had no information about him. I was terribly worried. I get the message by phone from my other best friend, Con Saggers, that Harry is okay. I'm going downstairs and will get more information about Harry from Con.

Thursday 12th September 1940.

Harry has left to join the Marines. I feel sorry about that. I couldn't say goodbye to him. And that's a great pity. Irene would have gone with me to a public bomb shelter. She didn't come, and I went to her house where I found her with Roy, a friend of hers and mine. We went for a walk.

On Brixton Road, we had a cup of coffee. My cup was half-filled when the sirens went off. So, we went back home, and she asked me if she, Irene with me and of course Roy could gondola our shelter. At first, I asked Mrs Williams for permission, and she agreed. So, I went for blankets, and we went into the bomb shelter. Later, we went to sleep, and Irene was laying in my arms. We stayed there until it calmed down a bit, that was at 16:45 pm, and then Irene and Roy went back home.

Sunday 15th September 1940

We've had five air-raid alarms. It was a hard night, and many bombs were dropped. We almost died for the second time. A bomb had fallen just along with our house, and the house opposite the street was destroyed. Fortunately, the people who lived there were not at home. They were in a bomb shelter with friends. It was a man with his wife and three children. The Germans dropped an enormous number of bombs on Brixton. Yesterday evening there were four of them fallen in our street, and our street isn't big. Most of all, the east of London is being bombed. All the people who live there are Jewish. A lot of them have died there.

Monday 16th September 1940

It's exactly 01:10 am, and we have had already three alarms... that day, we've had another three.

Tuesday 17th September 1940

Today we've had five air-raid alarms.

Wednesday 18th September 1940

It's now exactly 12:45 pm, and they just gave the 5th siren. Today there will probably be a record of air-raid sirens. They now gave a total of eight alarms. There are new messages that the airport of Deurne-South has been bombed. I hope it will be there as it was when I left.

Thursday 19th September 1940

Today it has been six weeks since I wrote to my family at home. I still didn't get an answer. This afternoon I will go to the place from where I've sent the telegram.

Friday 20th September 1940

We have had two air-raid alarms.

Saturday 21st of September 1940

Again we have had two air-raid alarms. In the evening, it's nine hours of alarms. It's enormous.

Sunday 22nd September 1940

Yesterday I had been to the hotel another time and helped do the dishes and other things. It cost me a shilling for all the buses I had to take. I thought I would get something for it, but they gave me nothing this time. Again, we've had three alarms. The last one started at 19:00 pm. It didn't stop until 02:30 am. Again, the Germans have dropped a lot of bombs.

Monday 23rd September 1940

Again we've had three air-raid alarms.

Tuesday 24th September 1940

Again three.

Wednesday 25th September 1940

We've just had two air-raid alarms. In the evening, I received a letter from my cousin Emanuel. He wrote to me that he would send me a postal parcel. I expect the parcel one of these days. The parcel should be five ties, a pullover, a sports jacket, underpants and a pack of cigarettes. He also wrote to me that if the sports jacket was too big, I should sell it.

He also wrote me something I didn't know. It will be New Year for the Jewish people next Tuesday. And on 12th October, it will be Jom Kippur. He wrote that New Year starts on Wednesday evening and the 1st and 2nd new year's days are on the 3rd and 4th of October. Now I've received the post parcel. I will send him an answer.

Today I went to my work, and it was terribly cold. Fortunately, I had my gloves with me, so it didn't bother me. But I had problems with the cold the day before yesterday. Then I didn't have my gloves with me. In the next letter that I will write to Cousin Emanuel, I'll ask him if his wife can knit a pair of mittens. It would be nice when I am on my bike.

Thursday 26th September 1940

Had a lot of air-raid alarms. There were six of them today.

Friday 27th September 1940

Again four of them. Planes above our house. We can't sleep in our house anymore.

Saturday 28th September 1940

Again we've had three air-raid alarms. I sleep already for three days in the shelter of Mr Benevente. This man is a Dutchman. He is one of the A.R.P.

Mrs Williams asked me for my money before she left home. The situation is terrible now in our house. This afternoon there will be no bread anymore, we are without food, and no bakery is open.

Sunday 29th September 1940

There is still no bread, and I go to work without eating. This afternoon I will get some French fries. It is 12:15 pm now, and we've already had two air-raid alarms. This amount has raised now to six.

Monday 30th September 1940

Today, a man offered me to come to live with him. It is one of our customers. He is a widower and has a shop of his own. I've been drinking tea with him several times.

Tuesday 1st October 1940

We have had five air-raid alarms.

Wednesday 2nd October 1940

We have had eight air-raid alarms today. So that's for the second time. I have been talking again with Mr Dennis, one of our customers, and he told me that he would get a room prepared for me. He hated the way it is with us now. I could come to him next Friday. Yesterday when I arrived home there was nothing left to put on my bread. Even there was no sugar anymore in my coffee. I hate it more and more. This evening I couldn't go for a walk with Irene because her soldier was with her.

Thursday 3rd October 1940

This morning again, I didn't have something to put on my bread, and even I couldn't drink the chocolate milk that I made because there wasn't a crumb of sugar anymore in the house. This afternoon I didn't take any food with me, and I will eat French fries again.

It is the end of the week, and I have incurred many costs already. This morning I started buying sardines. I could buy that for my 15/ [75p]. Now I must go at lunchtime to Woolworth, a shop like in Belgium, the Sarma, and I will buy a scouring pad for my hands, a washcloth to wash myself, and a scarf, a silk one. It is for the daughter of Mrs Benevente.

Next Sunday, she will turn 28 years old. The Benevente family are so nice to me. I want to give their daughter a little present. Mrs Benevente is a Christian woman, just like Mrs Zomerplaag, and knows everything about Judaism. When she married her husband, she became Jewish. She speaks Dutch very well, even though she's only visited Holland for fourteen days. Sheba speaks very good German, and that's why she learned Dutch so well. She herself is an English woman.

Other costs are two lights for my bike and a hand brake. That's easier for me. A suitcase that cost me 36 francs. A pair of overshoes for 25 francs. And tonight, I will go to a public bathhouse and want to wash myself in a good way, as I haven't had a bath in three weeks. Altogether, we are an amount of precisely 15/ [75p]. I've saved 17/ [85p], So that will be all right. I still am saving money for my holiday to go to Belgium when the war is over. It's almost time for me to go shopping, so I will stop now.

Friday 4th October 1940

Five times we have had an air-raid alarm.

Saturday 5th October 1940

Six times we have had the alarms.

Sunday 6th October 1940

We've had five air-raid alarms. In the evening, I was at Irene's home and met her brother Harry. He's a nice boy, very friendly.

Monday 7th October 1940

We've had seven air raid alarms today. During lunchtime Con and I have been to the movies. It was very nice.

Tuesday 8th October 1940

Today we've had six air-raid alarms. This morning the Germans have thrown bombs on Covent Garden. There were six bombs. This time I thought I was done, but fortunately, the bombs were falling in front of the market and on the backside. This afternoon I went to the Regal and have seen two nice movies. One was 'Private Detective 'and the other one 'My Two Men'. It was very amusing.

Thursday 10th October 1940

This morning we were able to eat just bread without anything on it. There was no butter, jam or anything else. When I came home this afternoon, the refugees were gone.so I went to my Dutch friends and told them everything. Mr Benevente told me that I had to pick up my belongings because he could have me in his home for a few days, and then he would try to put me in a boys house, or otherwise, I could go to his daughter in Camberwell.

Saturday 12th October 1940

So this afternoon, I moved to Camberwell. It's lovely there. The food is fantastic, and the house is very clean. I am there with a boy, an orphan of 18. Tomorrow I will go out with him. He is smaller than I am.

Sunday 13th October 1940

This afternoon I went with Sid to the cinema. The movies were not so special. Until today, from last Monday on, we have had thirty-six air raid alarms...

Above us lives a woman. She is 20 and next month she is expecting a baby. Her husband is 50+. It's not too bad. On the second floor, there lives a widow with her two daughters. One is 23, and the other is 27. Very nice people.

Saturday 19th October 1940

This afternoon I have been for the first time to Groveway and picked up my letters there. I've received a letter with an insurance card in it. I can go to a doctor without paying now. They take money directly from my salary.

I also visited Mr and Mrs Benevente, she was happy to see me and gave me a kiss. I saw Emile for more than an hour and went back to Mr and Mrs B and drank tea with them.

Sunday 20th October 1940

It's again Sunday, and I've been working today. We went to get wood in Clapham. We left our bikes there and came home with a barrow full of wood. Then we brought back the barrow, picked up our bikes, and it was already too late to go to the movies. This week in total, we have had thirty-one air-raid alarms. I didn't hear much but what I've heard yesterday and today is that nineteen bombs were thrown nearby. That's not okay.

Monday 21st October 1940

I think I've nothing to report. Now that the air-raid is over, I can go home and have a warm dinner.

Saturday 26th October 1940

Saturday morning, I almost died because there were thrown three bombs on Covent Garden without an air-raid alarm. I heard the bomb whistle; people fell to the ground, and people were running away from the explosion. I thought this time it would strike me. I had just missed out, and I thought the next would clock on my head.

Sunday 27th October 1940

For the first time since I left home, I felt very sad. I even have done something I never do at all; I've cried. You shouldn't think something like that from a naughty boy like me.

Monday 28th October 1940

Late in the afternoon again, I have been with Sid to the movies. There was a nice movie with Ronald Colman, and to my great pleasure, I noticed that I could understand more and more from the movies. I am happy about it.

In the evening we have had a lot of pleasure at home. Gladys was with us, and it became a cosy evening.

Every morning when I go to work, I give and I get a kiss from Mrs Branson. The same happens when I go to sleep.

It is starting to become very cold in England, and I will need gloves and a bearskin for my ears and face.

This week we have had thirty-two air-raid alarms. So that's one more than last week.

Tuesday 29th October 1940

Today the Germans have thrown a bomb again. It seems to be a very close burst that was not so bad this time. It was close to Waterloo Station.

Now we have air raid alarms for more than 13 hours. That's a long time, isn't it? Yesterday I played as a hairdresser. I have washed my hair of Gladys with shampoo. The payment came later...

Sunday 3rd November 1940

Unexpected Irene came to visit me. We had a nice day. We keep together. I mean as good as girl and boy. She continues to charm my heart. It's for more than five months now that I have known her. She brought me a jacket for when I'm riding the bike. It's one of her sisters.

Next Sunday I'm going to visit her, and I must spend money on some presents. I will give flowers to her mother, for her, I buy winter socks, and I give her sister something for the household because she's going to marry next week.

Monday 4th November 1940

This night, I meant last night. It was the quietest night since 7th September. Not one time, the Germans came over. But it was terrible weather.

Tuesday 5th November 1940

The air raid alarms this night took 14 hours and five minutes. It was the longest one until now. How early it becomes dark now, how earlier the alarm goes off and will end late the next morning.

Saturday 9th November 1940

This afternoon I visited Madame Catlin in their new home. The weather was bad, and I was sleeping there too. It's a nice house but a little bit far away.

Sunday 10th November 1940

We've only had one air raid alarm. That makes twenty-four this week. That's the least number of all these past weeks. The weather is now very cold. But still, it's not the winter weather that the people in England are used to. My best friend Con is going this week to the marines, army or air force. I think he will go into the air as a pilot or machine gunman.

Saturday 16th November 1940

This afternoon I went with Mr Branson to a good shop and bought myself trousers and pyjamas. The trousers costed me 16/6 d [83p] and the pyjamas 6/11 [34p]. The trousers cost me in Belgian money, about 99 francs before the war and the pyjamas 35 francs. Now there is really nothing to report except that we are doing well in Greece. The Italians get really giddy there. In a few years, I will have to fight in the war for mama and Fre. I don't care about that, but sure we will win this war. The English people would rather kill themselves than have to live under the rules of Mr Hitler.

Sunday 17th November 1940

There's nothing new to report. In one week, we've had twenty-three air-raid alarms. I get less and less as the weather gets worse. That's all we wish in the evening. This week a pilot of the air force earned the Victoria cross because while he fell, he managed to take his opponent down. One of our Spitfires, that's the name of our fighter planes, met on his patrol a Messerschmitt 110 and got involved in combat. The pilot of our plane was hit in his thigh, got a shard in his eye and his petrol tank was hit. Soon the plane was on fire. While he tumbled down, the pilot fired at the Messerschmitt and saw, to his surprise, the other plane tumbled into the sea. He himself, I mean our pilot, jumped out of the plane with his parachute and landed on the ground. He was taken to a hospital, and there the doctors feared for his life. Now he is stable but is still in the hospital.

The record of taking down enemy aircraft in a single day was set a few months ago, with one hundred and eighty-seven taken down on the day the Germans wanted to attack us.

Saturday 23rd November 1940

This afternoon I visited the refugees. When I talked with Edward, he told me that Florrie, the second girlfriend that I had in England, works in Brixton market. Later I went there, and I brought her home. She was happy that I was fine.

Sunday 24th November 1940

Today I have a bad day, and I am in a bad mood. I didn't amuse myself not at all today. In the whole week, we've had eighteen air-raid alarms. It has diminished significantly.

Monday 25th November 1940

Today I spoke with Mr Conway. He is a good friend of mine with a lot of money. The business Tirunelveli & Co is his. He wanted to give me 1 shilling, but I said I don't want money but a shirt. He went with me to the cafe and gave 10/- [50p] to Con to buy a shirt for me.

This Saturday, instead of one shirt, I'm going to buy two shirts if I added 2/ [10p] from my clothing allowance. So that's my first present.

Wednesday 27th November 1940

I've been to the Red Cross, and they told me that I couldn't get an answer yet because of the simple reason that there were no answers from Belgium yet.

Saturday 30th November 1940

This afternoon I've been to the afternoon classes for the purpose of air protection, and I have spent several hours there attentively, learning all about the gases. We were permitted to smell a few gases. Also, I've got a lesson on how to put a gas mask on quickly. Now I can become a messenger of the air protection. I will get then 2/6d [12p] per month plus the use of the bike.

Sunday 1st December 1940

This afternoon I went walking with Gladys again. Later in the afternoon, we went to sit lovely in Lyons and had coffee with a pastry. And it wasn't expensive at all.

We have had in the last week just twenty-two air-raid alarms. It becomes very calm; the Germans seem to have almost had enough of London. They are bombing now other cities because our defences are most effective. They are still losing enough planes every time they fly over. And if you hear the messages in Dutch on radio Hilversum, then you know what a liar they are. We must win this war. There's nothing to do about that.

Monday 2nd December 1940

Yesterday evening I went with Mr Branson to the air defence. I have been sitting there for a while and played billiards with another messenger. I beat him 101-63. You can see what kind of player I am. I've got from Mr Sutton, the leader there, a little booklet with lots to sell for Christmas. I think I can sell tomorrow at least seven items in Covent Garden.

Tuesday 3rd December 1940

As I thought, I've sold lots today, but I hadn't thought that I would have sold out by 10 o'clock. I've sold twenty in total. This evening I will ask for another booklet. It was a good start for me.

Yesterday we didn't have any air-raid alarms either at night or during the day. That's a good sign. I started today with the shopping; I mean in our office. If only I persist now.

Wednesday 4th December 1940

Today I've sold twenty lots again. It's the most of all there is sold. Today I've had the worst day that I have experienced in England. It started this morning with forgetting my handkerchief, I didn't have lights on my bike, so I had to walk ten minutes to the tram because I travel cheaper then. I was twenty-two minutes late for work. I lost my sunglasses when I was on my bike, and when I came home in the afternoon, I fell asleep on the tram and missed my stop. Then I had to come back for money, so I didn't save money at all. I left in the tram my school bag, in it was my raincoat, a book, apples, gloves.

Thursday 5th December 1940

Fortunately, I've got back my school bag at the tram depot. It took me 3 francs again.

Friday 6th December 1940

I've nothing to tell you today.

Saturday 7th December 1940

This afternoon I've been in the room with the gases. First, I didn't cry, but after half an hour, it started a little bit, and after an hour, the tears rolled down my face.

Sunday 8th December 1940

Yesterday we didn't have any air-raid alarms at night nor during the day. Today the sirens went off for the first time at 5:30 am. There were ten alarms this week. I think that's very good. Other cities got a lot more, for instance, the city of Cousin Emanuel and its surrounding. But most of all, it was in Bristol.

Monday 9th December 1940

I've told you that yesterday we had the siren at 5:30 am, but it became a terrible night. At 11:00 pm, I woke up, and I kept watch at the door in case of fire. I kept watching from 11.00 pm until 2.00 am in the morning. Then the worst was over. I've heard falling and whistling a terrible number of bombs. A lot of firebombs were thrown, and there were a lot of fires.

(They are boars, the Germans)

Saturday 14th December 1940

Today I've been for the last time to my training course for a messenger of the air protection. Last week we were to and in the room to learn about the gas.

Sunday 15th December 1940

In the whole week, there were eight air raid alarms. But neither heavy nights nor many bombs were thrown. Today is, or it was, the birthday of Rudolf Hardijzer.

This afternoon I've been to the movies. I've seen the movie: 'Only angels have wings, with Gary Grant and Jean Arthur. It was a very nice movie. Yesterday morning I brought Mr Russell, who lives above us, to the train. First, we took the underground train. It was for the first time that I had been there. I like it very much.

Monday 16th December 1940

Today I'm sixteen years old for the first time in my life abroad, but with very good people. It's still in the morning, and I've not seen any present. Just from Con Saggers, I've got money to buy a tie, because the tie of Madame and Mr Vieyra is worn out.

Tuesday 17th December 1940

Yesterday evening at the table Mr and Mrs Bransom gave me the presents from the closet. From Syd, the other boy, I've received light for my bicycle. I got a nice green tie from Mrs Bransom, that fits very good with the shirt that I bought with the money Mr Conway gave me. From Mr Bransom, I got a nice pair of socks. Also, there was a letter from Cousin Emanuel. He has moved because he has had firebombs on his house, and now he has a little villa, and it's even cheaper. He didn't send me anything because he has a very bad time now. The business has come to an end because the trades with Holland and France are finished now. We hope for better times for him and for all of us. Just before the meal, Gladys came in, and she gave me very nice handkerchiefs. I really needed some. I only had in my closet the six handkerchiefs which I took with me from home. Even a nice birthday, although in wartime.

The air raid alarms are decreasing. Yesterday evening there were two of them. One was at 21:45 pm for ten minutes and one from 22:15 just for five minutes. Mussolini was already beaten, and Hitler got his part within a short time.

Friday 20th December 1940

Since Sunday I haven't spent one cent on sweets. Now it's Friday morning. So that's in total and a record for me, up to 4 days.

Sunday 22nd December 1940

The amount of air-raid alarms this week was five.

Wednesday 25th December 1940

Yesterday was Mr Bransom's birthday. I've given him a nice tie with a little handkerchief for in his vest. Today it's Christmas, and we have a little party. In England, Christmas is celebrated in grand style.

I've given Mrs Bransom a hot water pot and a silk handkerchief. For Syd, I have bought a bracelet with his name and address on it. Last week I bought one for myself. For Mrs Benevente I've bought a little box with chocolate and for Gladys a scarf of silk. Mr and Mrs Bransom got me a tie.

Thursday 26th December 1940

This afternoon we went to Mrs Benavente. From there we went to the parents of Mr Bransom and have been eating their sandwiches with apricots. We were back home at 20:00 pm, and then we went to the party in the A.R.P. I drank cider and beer together and port. Much to my regret, I had to go home at 22:30. Of course, I was the only one. Mrs Bransom came home at 3:00 am. A man called my name at the party to sing, but I refused, I'm too shy. I like to sing at the A.R.P. If there are no strangers.

Yesterday and today, there was no work. It's also very quiet at my work. One of these months, maybe we all will get fired. Then I'm sure that I'm joining the air force and will study to be a pilot. That's all I must report now.

Friday 27th December 1940

We've had an air raid again in the evening. Until 11:00pm. Again, there were thrown a lot of firebombs.

Saturday 28th December 1940

Again there was no air-raid alarm in the evening. That makes four evenings this week.

Sunday 29th December 1940

Over the week, we have had a total of three alarms. I think it will become better slowly. We've been to Clapham and spent the afternoon there. In the evening, there was an air-raid alarm, and we went back home by bus. It was a heavy evening, and I had to do my first message for the A.R.P. post. On my way, I had to tumble down four times. At 23:30 pm, the alarm finished. However, they have caused fires that lasted more than 14 hours. I think that one of these days, I will become a diamond cutter. I can make more money then. I will hear tomorrow at the place where the refugees are working. As I've heard, there is a man from the Muggenberglei. His name is

Cardozo. Maybe I know him. I'll write more details in my report the day after tomorrow.

Tuesday 31st December 1940

I've been to the refugees. The first known face that I saw when I entered was Albert Nabarro. Then I saw Mr Swalef from the Provinciestraat, the butcher. I went to him, and he told me that Bill Boutwille was in England. I was totally amazed. He gave me the address of his work and later I would go there. First, I talked with the boss, and he noted my name to come to work with him in three weeks' time. Then I went to see Bill. He worked not far away at all, at Japie Van Der Wieken. When I came upstairs, Bill was so shocked that, at first, he couldn't say anything.

Saturday 18th January 1941

The third brother was in America. The fourth brother is dying in Poland. Then the Germans come to offer a nice medal to the mother for the brave behaviour of her son in Poland. At the end of the film, the mother is going to America, together with her daughter in law, where her son is waiting for her. Beautiful, it made me cry.

The second film was with Robert Young and Maureen Sullivan. About horse races and a lot of nice stories. Next week there is to see: Strike up the band, a beautiful film with Micky Roonie and Judy Garland. But first I need to have enough money so I can go there.

Sunday 19th January 1941

I have been at the post this morning from 09:00 till 13:00 pm and in the evening from 19:45 pm till 21:15 pm. We've had seven air-raid alarms this week, however non-heavy. Yesterday evening my shoes came back. Every two months, I must repair my soles and heels. I walk a lot, and I just have one pair of good shoes.

They're not going to change me from one A.R.P. post to another. All the people from the A.R.P. have received a raincoat for their work. I now need one, but I don't get one because I'm a messenger. I get a cape, that's yellow trousers with a yellow jacket and a yellow hat for when I'm on the bike during the rain. It's a pity, but I'm already happy that I get something.

Monday 20th January 1941

In the whole week, we've had seven air-raid alarms. Again, non were heavy.

Tuesday 21st January 1941

Today is mama's birthday. I hope she was able to experience it. I wish mama and Fre congratulations on mama's birthday. When the war is over, Mama and Fre will get their presents. I will see to it.

Saturday 25th January 1941

This afternoon I went with Albert Nabarro to the movies. We've seen two nice films. I had almost there a girl around my neck out of stupidity. Afterwards, I regretted not going for it. It doesn't matter. Next Sunday I will go out again with Albert. Then we will meet other girls. For the last three months, I've not been interested in girls. But now it comes up again.

Next Saturday there's football. 1st February, Belgium vs Holland, or Holland vs Belgium. We don't know exactly what it is, because the match will be played in England. On Thursday, I've been to Mr Obstfeld and talked with him about the cutting of diamonds. It won't take long anymore, up to two weeks. Then we get at least a bit more salary to start than that what we got here at Monro for the youngest servant and clerk at the same time.

Sunday 26th January 1941 Sunday

Generally, we've got in the whole week four air-raid alarms. On Tuesday three times and Wednesday, just the once. I expected already a heavy attack on Sunday because Hitler loves Sundays, but it didn't come. They are preparing for an invasion. It won't be two years before we have won.

Monday 27th January 1941

This afternoon I've got money at the diamond cutters. I've got 2/ [10p]from Bill, 1/ [5p]from Mr Van der Wieken, 2/ [10p] from Joske Abrahamson, 1/ [5p]from David Vleeschdrager and 1/ [5p] from the adjuster. That makes 7/ [35p] in total. It's more than my pocket money. The biggest part is of course for my clothes.

Sunday 6th April 1941

The second film was:" Sherlock Holmes", with Basil Rathbone. Yesterday he was a killer today. He was a detective. This week we've had four air-raid alarms. None was heavy or took a long time. That is now 12 days of silence. He must be thinking about something else than about us: Yugoslavia.

Sunday 13th April 1941

We've had seven air-raid alarms this week.

Wednesday 16th April 1941

This evening we've had a violent air-raid...

Thursday 17th April 1941

...which lasted until the next morning, I mean lasted until 5:00 am today. It was the most violent attack yet. A lot of bombs, but fortunately, I'm still alive. I walk around the streets to see if everyone is healthy, I mean, okay. I don't have any work because there is no electricity. This afternoon I've been to the movies to see: 'Spring Parade' and 'The Son of Monte Cristo'.

Friday 18th April 1941

There is still no work, but I received my full salary. I've only worked for two days. Monday, I didn't work because it was Easter. Next week and the week after next week, we will be working overtime. Then everything is okay.

Saturday 19th April 1941

This evening again, a violent air attack. This time a lot of firebombs and explosion bombs.

Sunday 20th April 1941

There were five air raid attacks, two of them heavy. This afternoon I've taken out a girl. Just for friendship, not like at home. Just for the company because I can't be alone. I get bored.

Sunday 27th April 1941

This week there were six air-raid alarms. Neither one of them took a long time nor was violent.

I'm sorry that I don't write a lot, but it's because I haven't kept my diary for four weeks. From the 6th April until 4th May.

Sunday 4th May 1941

The weather is beautiful, and I've never felt so happy as today. I mean, since I've been in England. This morning I had an appointment with two girls from the chocolate shop. One of them, June, is working there, she or one of the other girls give me always extra because I'm a regular customer but most of all I am a good friend. But I didn't see them, so that saved me some money.

This afternoon I should go out with the daughter of a female warden, but she wasn't on time. The appointment was at 15:15 pm. I waited until 15:25, and then I went to the Camberwell Palace. She told me she had been there too but downstairs, and I was sitting upstairs. I've seen: 'The girl Downstairs', with Franchot Tone and Franciscan Gaal. The other film was: 'Stand up and Fight' with Robert Taylor and Wallace Beery.

The girl was there at 15:30 pm, but as you will know by now, I don't have patience, especially not for waiting on somebody. This week there was one air-raid alarm. That was yesterday evening. But nothing happened. I forgot to tell you that I had a party yesterday evening at Sid's aunt's house.

I went to bed at 3:20 am. I remembered that the clocks had been reset, so we have light until 10:00 am, next month until 11:00 am, which is practical.

This evening I've been to the movies, and I've seen Marlene Dietrich and John Wayne in 'Seven Sinners'. The Seven Sinners is the name of the cafe. The other film was: 'Charlie Chan in 'the Wax Museum' with Sidney Toler.

Hey, now I'm up to date again with my diary.

Saturday 10th May 1941

Today it's been a year since the war has started for us. As a remembering, I've taken some pictures of myself this morning... this evening I've been out with my girl. Her name is June, in fact, Juphemia. A lovely girl. She is one month younger than I am. I had known her already since March 1941. This evening I've taken her out to the Empress Theatre, and we've seen a wonderful performance. I had a good time. I have brought June back home, and it was 23.00 pm when I went to my house. Just when I got on the tram, the air raid alarm started. When I came home, it wasn't so bad. I went to bed and tried to sleep. At 00.30 am I came out of my bed and got dressed. It was too heavy to many bombs. So, I was dressed at 00.40 am.

Sunday 11th May 1941

When I came upstairs and investigated the garden, there came something out of the air, very close by. I called the man who stood at the front door, but he didn't hear me. I took to the street, and I heard that some wardens of the A.R.P. were wounded. One was lying next to the entrance of the park. I thought it was a soldier but, on his shoes, I saw it was Mr Bransom. He lay there groaning, and when I, crying, went to our post, they took him away with an ambulance. Then I went to the hospital with Mr Russell and visited Mr Bransom. I found him finally, and he was lying in his bed, quietly asleep. I stayed there for a while and did help the nurses and doctors to undress the wounded people. Later, I went to the Salvation Army, and I saw there Mrs Bransom together with all the people on our street. Sid was also hurt. He was lying in his bed and got some glass in his arm that came from the window.

At 04:30 am this morning, it was quiet for a while, and I went back to our post to drink my first cup of tea. I was so tired that I fell asleep sitting at the table. They brought me to bed. At 08.20 am, I came out of my bed, washed myself a little bit and went to the Police Station to hear in which room Mr Bransom was lying. Then I went back to the hospital and have seen Mr Bransom. He was much better. Then I went home. I saw Mrs Bransom, and I told her for the first time that her husband was hurt and where she could find him. Of course, she started crying and went to the hospital.

Now we are going to live at her mother's house until she has found a house. Mr Bransom will be transferred to a hospital in Leatherhead.

Monday 22nd May 1941

This afternoon I've been to the park with my girlfriend.

Wednesday 24th May 1941

Today I've been out with my tutor Bill Boutelje. First, I've been with him to Lyons Corner House, and we had a drink there. He hadn't eaten yet. Then we went for a walk, and at 12:15 pm we went to a Jewish restaurant to eat something. It was at Kahn. First, I took an hors d'oeuvre, then a chicken soup for the first time since I was in England. Then potatoes with the whole Breast of a chicken and a glass of beer. I could not eat a dessert anymore. Then we watched the football, Millwall vs Arsenal. The final score was 2-5. A fantastic match.

Afterwards, we went to watch 'Wildman of Borneo' starring Frank Morgan. The second film was 'The Fighting 69th', with James Gagne, Pat O'Brien and George Brent.

Then we went back to Piccadilly, and we were again at Lyons. Wonderful music and a lot of people. Again, I took a large hors d'oeuvre and sandwiches and had a cup of tea. Then I had to go home. It was time to go. Yesterday I was one year in England.

Thursday 25th May 1941

This afternoon I've been to see Mr Bransom in the hospital. He is looking good and will come home shortly.

Wednesday 31st May 1941

This afternoon I've been again to Mr Bransom. In the evening I've been with June to the movies. We saw two funny movies. The first one was: 'Bank Detective' and the other was 'Marx Brothers Go West.

Thursday 1st June 1941

Today I went out with Bill. First, we were going to Richmond, we had lunch there, and afterwards, we went rowing. Later we went to a tearoom where we had tea with some pastries. We went back to the subway.

Then we went to Marble Arch Corner House, also again Lyons, where I've had hors d'oeuvres with sandwiches and beer. Afterwards, we had coffee and ice cream. After this, we went for a walk, and I went back home on the tube.

Friday 2nd June 1941

This morning I had a discussion about certain matters, which gave us a different idea about ourselves.

This afternoon I've been to the movies, and the two films were: 'The Saint's Vacation', with Sally Grey and Hugh Sinclair and: 'You Will Find Out', with Kay Keyser, Boris Karloff and Peter Lorre. For the past three weeks, we haven't had any air raid alarm. Just now and again, an alarm at 12:10 am.

Thursday 8th June 1941

I went out with that girl again today, also her friend and another boy. We've seen: 'Jessy James', with Tyrone Power, Henry Fonda, Nancy Kelly and Randolph Scott.

13th June 1941 (I forgot this)

I've received good news this morning. The people from Preso, who were in Toulouse, received a letter from their father and father in law, in which it was written that my mother was asking for me. That same afternoon I sent a telegram to her, and in the evening, I was permitted to eat in the Dutch House that was liquidated. I've written a letter by airmail. Let's hope for the best.

Wednesday 14th June 1941

I've been out again with Bill today. We went to one of the best movie theatres in Leicester Square and have seen there: 'Bittersweet', with Jeannette Mac Donald and Nelson Eddie. Afterwards, we went to a cafe and drank far too much. I got drunk, but not so drunk that I didn't know what I did. I wanted to be drunk. That's why I did it. I finally went to bed at 03.00 am.

Thursday 15th June 1941

From that place, we went to Golders Green. It's a place where rich Jewish people live, and we've looked there for a place for Bill. We had a nice meal in that neighbourhood, and later we went to the movies. The first film was: 'Man about town', with Jack Benny and Dorothy Lamour. The second was: 'Escape from yesterday', a Russian film.

We came home in the evening at 9.45, and I had been away from yesterday morning at 10.00 o'clock. I've held out well, didn't I!

18th June 1941

For the first time this year, I went swimming in Kensington Park. It's quite cold.

19th June 1941

This day, six years ago since my father died.

21st June 1941

Today it's a real summer's day. That's why I got out of my bed at 7.00 am, took the bus and went swimming in Rockwell Park. Wonderful place to swim. But not too big. I must say that since Monday we've had beautiful weather every day. Very warm and not nice to work.

16th June 1941 (Forgotten)

Bill and I went to a Dutch Emergency Committee of which Mrs Kiek (unknown) is the head. She gave me a voucher for clothes. I went to that place with Bill, and there was a friend of Bill, a man named Van Praag, and of course, he gave me the best clothes. I've got: a wonderful grey suit, a pair of shoes that were second hand, two beautiful shirts (21/.),£1.05p and two pairs of underpants and vests, one pair of pyjamas, a waistband, two pairs of silk socks, one t-shirt and a sport shirt. It all comes from the Dutch Committee, although I'm not actually entitled to it.

27th June 1941

My last girlfriend and I made up again.

29th June 1941

Today I was in Banstead with Bill. A town outside London. I've been swimming there and have swam 100 yards in 90 seconds. That was my first training for the swim match of the A.R.P., Which will take place on 16th July. Also, we have twice had a good meal in Banstead.

3rd July 1941. I received a letter from my sister Fre to her beloved brother. She asked where was I living?

In the letter, she sends 1000 kisses, I will write a letter back to France, and they will forward it to Belgium.

28th June 1941

I forgot to write that on that Friday. I've got a .50p raise. Now I have £ 2 and about £ 1 tips from the boys because I get the tea for them. Very good for a boy of 16.

4th of July 1941

Today people from the Dutch paper Vrij Nederland (free Holland) came to our work and took some pictures that will appear in the paper. They took three pictures of me especially, and I'm sure that one of those three will appear in the paper, as I am the youngest of the staff.

12th July 1941

I've been together with Bill and the Benavente family to discuss the topic that was raised by Mr Boutelje. He wants me to become his adopted son. Of course, it's difficult to leave the Bransom family, but I will get clothes, a bicycle, a dog, everything that I want. And, I can save more money to give to my mother and Fre when I will return to them. So, I think I will go.

12th July 1941

Later in the afternoon, I went swimming. On the way, there was a massive thunderstorm which was terrible, and my clothes were totally wet right through. It's the first time that it's been raining since 16th June. I've trained again and have broken my record. I only swam 40 yards in 30 seconds.

13th July 1941

I've been swimming again today, and I had a nice day. We were with the five of us. Two girls and three men.

16th July 1941

Today I am 16 years and 7 months. As a present, I took a day off, because I am going swimming this evening. I did swim the Messengers race and came 2nd. The first place was a champion of our district. I've also won in the redemption race, and we were first against the Home Guards and others. We were in last place in the final race. We lost against the Police, who had the most points, and the firemen. In fact, it was very good because we were with three of the four who were under 18 years, and the firemen and policemen were all adults, just like the Home Guards.

I had second place in the Messengers race, and for that, I won a medal.

14th July 1941

For the second time, I broke up with June.

26th July 1941

This evening I am dancing with my friend George and his friend Ken. These two boys couldn't dance...

27th July 1941

...at all. I could dance the Slow Walz and the Quick-Step. I had a good time. That's the first time I've really been to a dance, especially with two friends. I danced with five girls and twice with the same girl.

28th July 1941

I got up this morning at 2.00 am because there was an air raid. It was the first one since 27th June. It lasted until 4.00 am but wasn't fierce. There was heavy anti-aircraft fire. I had to watch an entire sector because there were not enough Wardens in the neighbourhood.

Friday evening, my holiday week begins, and Mr Boutelje and I are going

Torquay. It's a seaside resort close to the neighbourhood of Cousin Emanuel. He is waiting for us as soon as we have time to visit his house.

30th July 1941

19th August 1941

Today it's the day that Fre becomes 19 years. That's why I want to congratulate her.

20th August 1941

This evening I went to a Civil Defence Ball. We didn't have such a good evening as on Saturday.

23rd August 1941

I danced again and had a good time. Unfortunately, I missed the last tram, so I came home at 1.00 o'clock instead of 12.00.

24th August 1941 Sunday

Today I've been out with my girlfriend. We walked, went to Lyons corner house, to the movies, and later on, we walked again.

27th August 1941

I've played cards this evening with the A.R.P [air raid protection team]. Card, but I've lost.

The evening before yesterday, I met two girls who were talking with two friends of mine, and they asked if it was possible to go dancing today in Peckham with the S.P. (Stretcher Party], ambulance team during air raids).

I was going and had a nice evening. I came back home at 12.00 o'clock. Mrs Bransom thought it was okay. She didn't say much.

29th August 1941

I've got today a raise in my salary again, 10/.[50p] It's the third time in 9 weeks that I've got more. It's a wonderful salary for a 16-years old boy.

30th August 1941

Today I went out with Bill today, and I wore my new suit, that I'm wearing for the first time. We've been to the Queen's party in Regents Park. Very interesting. And at Kahn's, I've eaten three plates of chicken soup. (Danced later until 11.00 o'clock.)

31st August 1941 Sunday

In fact, it is Queens day, a special day in Holland, but in England, it's very quiet on Sunday. The busiest day is here on Saturday. The whole day and evening I was with my girlfriend, and I didn't spend any money. I mean only for the tram. My girlfriend doesn't like tearooms. She doesn't feel comfortable there.

6th September 1941

I've been to the Coöp dance hall. That's a place where I will regularly go dancing. We had a good time.

7th September 1941 Sunday

I went out with my girlfriend.

13th September 1941

I've been to the Coöp again.

14th September 1941

I had made an appointment with my girlfriend. I didn't go there (for a certain reason), so now I have finished again with this one (4 weeks). I've been to a social dance event.

18th of September 1941

This afternoon I've been to Stratton House to send a telegram to Belgium. The girl that helped me there was totally surprised because mama had written to the Consul of Lisbon and had asked them where I was. The girl had been looking for me for six months, and she never found me. She had a lot of letters and answers, but they were all from other people with the name Muller, and now I've come here myself. She would just try in East Indies.

I was swimming for 15 minutes this afternoon, and this evening I've been to the movies with one of our young A.R.P. girls who are since a short time on our post.

19th of September 1941

This evening I've been to the Coöp. It was there a communist dance event. It's not about politics. It's about the dance. I've brought home one of the girls who was wearing an evening dress.

20th of September 1941

I've been to the Coöp.

21st of September 1941, Sunday

I've been to the A.R.P. dance event and had a really good time. In the evening I've been to another dance, but it was so crowded there that I went home quite early.

22nd of September 1941

I didn't go to work because of the Jewish New Year had begun (5702.). Because the family in Belgium or Holland cannot go to the synagogue to pray there, I didn't go to work, and I've been to the synagogue myself. I hope and wish at the same time that mama and Fre and the whole family are okay and that the war will soon be over so that we will be able to stay together very soon.

23rd of September 1941

Today, it's exactly one year and four months that I have been staying in England. I bought a hat. A wonderful hat. It fits very well with the nice suit that I've bought 4 weeks ago and which I wrote about, I believe.

1st of October 1941

Today it's Yom Kippur, and I've fasted from yesterday evening from 6:15 until 7:15 today. I didn't feel anything from it.

4th of October 1941

I've been dancing at the Coöp.

5th of October 1941, Sunday

I've been dancing at the A.T.C. School.

Mrs Bransom has had a baby. It's a girl, and they have called her Rita.

There was an A.R.P. dance event from our post. I was introduced to a girl, and of course, she became my girl. She is 22 years old. Her name is Reggie.

11th of October 1941

I've been dancing at the A.T.C. school. We call that the Labour Party dance. (Socialist).

17th of October 1941

There's not so much to tell. I don't want to write about this time of war. I've been to the Coöp again. And it was again a socialist event.

18th of October 1941

I've been to the Coöp. There was a Foxtrot competition. There was a wonderful couple who danced there.

19th of October 1941

I've written to France again. From there, they will send the letter forward to Belgium.

We played football. We lost 5-0. They had different players from clubs. Post 64- Post 26 was 5-0. Went to the Labour Party dance again.

23rd of October 1941

Today I'm 1 year and 5 months in England. Went dancing with Reggie.

24th of October 1941

Again I've lost a girl. Number 19. I've been dancing at the Coöp. Communist dance event.

25th of October 1941

I was playing football, and the final score was 1-1. I hurt my foot a little bit, and instead of going dancing, I went to bed early.

26th of October 1941, Sunday

I've had a good rest. Went to the Labour Party dance event. In the evening I went to the Loughborough Hotel and danced there. But it was not good.

27th until 31st of October

Nothing to write about.

1st of November 1941

I went to the dentist this afternoon, and he has pulled a tooth. In the evening, I danced, but I shouldn't have done that because my mouth was bleeding the whole evening.

2nd of November 1941, Sunday

I danced at the A.T.C., and in the evening, I went to the Loughborough Hotel. It was much better than last week.

3rd of November 1941

Today I had a lot of pain in my tooth, and in the evening, the dentist pulled out a tooth again.

5th of November 1941

There was a ball of the Fire Brigade. There were 750 people. It was terrible: too many people.

7th of November 1941

I've been to the Conservative Club. In the evening at the Loughborough Hotel. I've been dancing this week so many times just because of boredom.

10th of November 1941

Today I bought a 9-carat golden signet ring for £ 2.10 [£2.50p]. I had my name engraved on it, so the total I had to pay was £ 3.-.-.

14th of November 1941

I had dinner with Bill Boutelje in the city. Afterwards, we went dancing, but it wasn't a fun evening.

19th of November 1941

We have been listening to 'Aida'. The female singer was ill, so we have heard aria's of 'Tosca', 'La Traviata', La Bohème' and 'Carmen'.

21st of November 1941

I've got a raise in my salary today of 10/ [50p]- and so I'm now earning £ 5.-.-. I've been to an A.T.C. dance event.

22nd of November 1941

First, we played football against the Fire Brigade, winning 7-3. I scored a goal. In the evening I went to the dance at the Labour Party. There were not too many people. I had a nice evening.

23rd of November 1941

I was at the Coöp, but it wasn't a good evening.

29th of November 1941

First, I've been to the A.F.S. dance until 9:00. I left there because I had an appointment with a couple of friends. So, I went to another place to meet them, and when I went to get my clothes, they had disappeared from the dressing room. A wonderful raincoat, a nice hat, a pair of leather gloves and a silk tie. Everything is as good as new. I had to walk back home in the rain.

30th of November 1941, Sunday

I've been playing football in the afternoon for the Bromar Club. It was the first time that we played together. We played against the A.T.C. That's a club where the boys learn about flying, becoming a pilot, or something else in the air. We lost the match 4-0. In the evening, I've been again to the Labour Party dance.

2nd of December 1941

I bought this evening a coat for £ 8-8-. £8. 40p]-. Terribly expensive.

5th of December 1941

I've been to the movies with Bill. We've seen a good propaganda film, '49th Parallel with Leslie Howard.

6th of December 1941

I've been to the Labour Party dance. It poured with rain. Later I had to go to St. Giles to get information about my coat. They told me to come back another time.

16th of March 1942

For the first time since the 6th of June, we've had an air raid alarm. It ended after 25 minutes. They didn't drop bombs.

17th of March 1942

I've been to St. Anthony Hall. I danced the kissing waltz with Milly.

20th of March 1942 (it's on with Milly)

I've been to the Coöp with Milly.

21st of March 1942

In the afternoon I've been to the football, Dulwich. Hamlet 2 - Metropolitan Police 4. A very bad match. At 6:00, I picked up Milly from her work in the evening. We drank tea at home. Afterwards, we've been to St. Anthony Hall.

22nd of March 1942, Sunday

In the afternoon I've been to the movies with Milly, afterwards tea. In the evening, L.P. dances. It has been a nice weekend.

24th of March 1942

To the movies with Milly. 'Dr. Jekyll and Mr Hyde'. A terrible film. Spencer Tracy played a double role. It was a good film but very creepy.

26th of March 1942

It's Bill's birthday. We've had dinner at Folman's. Then we went by taxi to the Stoll Theatre. We've seen a nice show.

27th of March 1942

Coöp with Milly.

28th of March 1942

Milly came to our home. We drank tea, and afterwards, we went dancing in St. Anthony Hall.

29th of March 1942

I played football, Bromar 1 - Picture Post 0. A good match. I went to my home with Milly, where we drank tea, and then the L.P. dance. My leg is stiff from the match

31st of March 1942

I've been to the movies with Milly.

2nd of April 1942

To St. Anthony Hall with Milly.

3rd of April 1942

It's 'Good Friday'. I've been to Milly's house. A gramophone evening. I've brought Milly home in the rain.

6th of April 1942

Easter. In the afternoon a walk. In the evening, the Coöp. On my own.

9th of April 1942

I broke up with Milly. She had sent me a short letter. Didn't give any reason why.

10th of April 1942

Coöp. Two bands. Had a good evening.

11th of April 1942

In the afternoon to the movies. 'Dive-bomber'. Nice film. In the evening, L.P. dance. I've brought Phyllis back home.

12th of April 1942, Sunday

In the afternoon I've been dancing in the Covent Garden Opera House. A beautiful hall. Very nice for the first time. In the evening, L.P. dance.

14th of April 1942

I've been to the movies. Not bad.

15th of April 1942

Coöp. A.R.P. dance from the Mayor. Not bad.

16th of April 1942

I've been to the Coöp with Doris. I have a terrible cold, but I made this appointment last Sunday.

17th of April 1942

I've received a raise of 10/. [50p] Now I'm earning £8.-.-. A fantastic salary, and if I'm going to make more and more, I will get another raise. I went to bed early, at 8:00, to heal my cold.

18th of April 1942

First I've been shopping with Bill. In the afternoon we've been to the football.

Chelsea 0 - Portsmouth 0. Very bad match for Premier League football. Next week there will be the semi-final for the Cup. In the evening, L.P. dance. I've brought Phyllis back home.

19th of April 1942, Sunday

In the afternoon to the Covent Garden Opera House. I had a very good time. It was a pity that I was all alone. I didn't know anyone there in the evening L.P. dance. I've brought Phyllis back home.

20th of April 1942

I've picked up Milly from work, and we are good friends again. I didn't see her since the 5th of April. I've promised that I will go to St. Anthony Hall on Thursday.

21st of April 1942

I've been to the movies.

23rd of April 1942

I've been to the Coöp. Very good.

25th of April 1942

For the third time, I've sent £5 to Holland. In the afternoon we've been watching football. Millwall 2 - Arsenal 2. A good match.

26th of April 1942, Sunday

In the afternoon I've been to the Covent Garden Opera House with my friend Johnny. In the evening to the L.P. dance. I've brought home Grace (23).

27th of April 1942

St. Giles Hall. A dance event for the R.A.F. Benevolent Fund. It was very good.

28th of April 1942

I've been to the movies with Grace. 'Paris Calling'. Today I received a message from mama. The address is in The Hague.

The 30th of April, 1942

Coöp.

1st of May 1942

Coöp.

2nd of May 1942

This afternoon I sent a message to mama. I bought a pair of shoes. Afterwards to the movies. In the evening to the Coöp. I've brought Irene back home.

3rd of May 1942

In the afternoon, I've been going out with Violet (21). Afterwards, we've been drinking tea at Lyons. In the evening we went walking to Forest Hill. At 11:00, I was going home.

5th and 6th of May 1942

Coöp.

7th of May 1942

After work, I go swimming for half an hour.

8th of May 1942

This evening I received £ 1 raise. That makes my salary £ 9.-.-. I had a suit made. It costs me £ 13.2.6. £13.12p]

In the evening to the Coöp. I've brought Kitty and Doris back home.

9th of May 1942

I had pictures taken, and from a little portrait of Fre, I made a bigger picture. In the afternoon to the movies. In the evening dancing.

10th of May 1942, Sunday

Today marks 2 years since Hitler launched an invasion of our country. Exactly one year ago, we had the worst air-raid alarm, and we were bombed away.

In the afternoon to the Covent Garden Opera House. In the evening, L.P. dance. I've brought back home Joan (20) and her sister. We've had 14 days of nice weather today for the first time. It's raining.

10th of June 1942

This afternoon I've been to the movies. 'The Next of King'. A wonderful film about the war. This evening I've put on my new A.R.P[air-raid protection]. uniform for the first time.

12th of June 1942

Coöp.

13th of June 1942

In the afternoon to the movies. In the evening to the Coöp. I've brought Trudy back home.

14th of June 1942, Sunday

In the morning, a meeting of the diamond trade. In the afternoon to the movies with Joan. Afterwards, we've been drinking tea at home. In the evening, we stayed at home, and I brought Joan back home.

16th of June 1942

I've received a letter from mama. Picked up and paid for my suit. In the evening, the Coöp. Brought Joan back home.

17th of June 1942

In the afternoon, I slept. In the evening to the Coöp. A lot of people there. The proceeds of the dances are going to the people who suffered damage in the unexploded bomb that went off last week.

18th of June 1942

In the late afternoon to the movies. This morning I received the letter from the tax authorities. I must pay £ 33..53p for the last 6 months. This evening the Myers park, a dance in the open air.

19th of June 1942

Today marks 7 years since my dad died. Because of that, I stayed at home, and Joan did come to visit me.

20th of June 1942

In the evening to the St. George Cathedral Hall. It wasn't nice.

21st of June 1942, Sunday

For the first time, I've put on my new suit. At 6:00 in the evening, I took it off. In the afternoon I've been with Joan to the movies. In the evening we did stay at home. The cheapest weekend in months.

22nd of June 1942

Today I still didn't work. We will start tomorrow, but we will get 33/ less.[£1.66p]

23rd of June 1942

Today I've started to work at the new factory, in the evening at the Co-op. I've brought Joan back home.

24th of June 1942

In the evening at Brockwell Park, dance in the open air. Also, not very nice. I've brought Joan back home.

26th of June 1942

Today we've received our salary. Instead of £ 9.-.-. I now received £ 7.10-. [£7.50] again. Still a good salary. In the evening, the Co-op. Didn't enjoy myself at all.

27th of June 1942

In the afternoon, I've been to the movies with Mrs Bransom. 'How green was my valley'. A fantastic film, very dramatic. In the evening, the Co-op. Brought Joan back home.

28th of June 1942, Sunday

In the afternoon I've been to the Covent Garden Opera House with Joan. In the evening to the movies, afterwards tea.

30th of June 1942

To the Co-op. Brought Joan back home.

1st of July 1942

I've been dancing in the open air in Brockwell Park. Afterwards at 11.00 to Soho because Bill had forgotten his wallet. We went for nothing. The door was closed.

2nd of July 1942

I've been to a dance with Joan and her sister. It was an event of Joan's company. Didn't enjoy myself.

3rd of July 1942

In the evening, I've been with Joan to the Co-op.

4th of July 1942

In the afternoon I've been to the movies, and in the evening to Joan's house. I stayed there until midnight.

5th of July 1942 Sunday

First I've been swimming in the morning. Afterwards, I had a meal with Joan's sister at the Milk bar because she was also in the swimming pool. In the afternoon, I took them both out. We've been to the movies. In the evening, I had dinner at their home. Afterwards, we've made a walk to Peckham Park.

6th of July 1942

In the evening, I've been out with Banny. He's on leave. First to the movies, and afterwards, I had dinner at his house.

7th of July 1942

Joan is ill. There is a problem with her stomach. The doctor has told her that it's due to the transition from day shift to night shift.

8th of July 1942

In the evening, I visited Joan and brought her cherries.

9th of July 1942

This morning I've been to the inspection for the R.A.F. Anyway, they will not draft me before I am 18 years.

7th of November 1942

In the afternoon to the football. Millwall 1 - Brentford 2. A good match, but the referee made a mess of it in the evening at the A.T.C.

dance. I didn't like it. I've brought Grace (18) back home. Joan is 21 years today.

8th of November 1942, Sunday

In the afternoon to the movies. In the morning, A.T.C. drills. Our flight 'B. Flight has won for the Mayor and the high officers of the R.A.F. In the evening, L.P. dance. Joan was there. I brought Joan and her sister after the dance to the tram, at the same time another girl, Betty (17), was waiting for me.

9th of November 1942

In the evening to the movies. Behind me, Marie O' Toole and June Morse were sitting. I didn't see this last one since Christmas last year. First, I've brought home Marie, afterwards June.

10th of November 1942

This evening I've been to the movies. 'My Gal Sal'.

11th of November 1942

Today there is a ceasefire. This evening there was a heavy fog. I couldn't see anything. There will have been a lot of accidents. All the people had to walk. Today it's Milly's birthday. Yesterday evening I received a message from mama and Fre.

12th of November 1942

St. Giles. Not bad. We were dancing for the benefit of the troops.

13th of November 1942

Today I've received £ 1.-.-. More on my salary. I now earn £ 10.10.[£10.50p]-. Today I was with Phyllis (20). Ann (twins) picked me up at the A.T.C., and we walked to Ruskin Park.

14th of November 1942

In the morning, I volunteered for the R.A.F. with the Dutch people. I've to come back on Wednesday. In the afternoon, I've been to the movies, and in the evening to the Co-op.

15th of November 1942

I've been to Kelley Airport with the A.T.C. It was terrible weather, so they didn't fly. In the evening I've been to C.P. Stones with my friend Dick. It was not nice.

17th of November 1942

Co-op. Winnie (20). I've made an appointment for the following Monday.

18th of November 1942

I've been going back to the Dutchmen in Arlington House. Next month I will have my examination.

19th of November 1942

Co-op. I have met Gilberte. A Belgian girl from Oostende. She is living here in Wimbledon.

In the afternoon I've been to the football. Chelsea 4 - Millwall 2. Two goals from Millwall were disallowed. It was very disappointing for Millwall, and so Chelsea scored another two goals later. In the evening, I went to the Co-op with Dick.

22nd of November 1942

In the afternoon I've been playing football. Effrontery 3 - Bromar 3. It has been very foggy. In the evening, L.P., I've brought Joan back home.

23rd of November 1942

I've been to the movies. A film about Coastal Command.

24th of November 1942

To the Co-op. Joan's handbag has been stolen. Also, another girl lost her handbag.

25th of November 1942

A.T.C. I've received the result of my arithmetic exam. I was second with 74.

28th of November 1942

In the afternoon I've been to the dentist with Joan. Afterwards, I bought her a handbag for her birthday. Then we went home, and we had a cup of tea, and after that, we've been to the Co-op to dance.

29th of November 1942, Sunday

In the afternoon I've been to the movies with Joan, Bill (R.A.F.) and his girlfriend. Afterwards, we had a meal, and then we went dancing in Brixton, Bal. de Danse.

30th of November 1942

Especially I've been going to the A.T.C. for an exam in Morse code. 6 words per minute. I think I've passed.

1st of December 1942

I've been to the movies. 'Who Done It' and 'The great Impersonation'. Very good.

4th of December 1942

A.T.C. After the lessons I met Marion and Joyce, Dick was with me.

5th of December 1942

In the afternoon I've been playing football. Again, we have won. B. Flight 343 - A Flight 343 9-4. I've made 1 goal in the evening L.P. dance. In between, I've been walking with Ann (twins).

7th of December 1942

J.W.A.O. dance for the prisoners of war. I've brought Connie (17) back home. She invited me to a party next Saturday, but I think I'm not going.

8th of December 1942

I had to go to Arlington House this afternoon. I had to wait two hours. When I finally came to the captain, he just spoke with me for two minutes. In the evening I've been to the movies. (brought Connie back home.)

9th of December 1942

When I came to present myself for the medical examination, they told me that they had received the papers from Cardington. So, my medical examination wasn't necessary anymore. I went back to Arlington House. The captain told me that I would enter service on the 16th of December. I quit my job today, 7 days.

10th of December 1942

I've had a cup of tea at Mrs Benavente's house. Afterwards, I've been to the movies with June (18). (1941).

11th of December 1942

I've been to the A.T.C. With Dick, I've met Connie and her girlfriend.

12th of December 1942

In the morning I buy a pair of shoes, in case I will get leave when I'm in the army. In the afternoon I've been playing football. Rosie House 1 - A.T.C. II. 7. I've scored two goals. In the evening, I've been to the Co-op with Joan.

13th of December 1942, Sunday

In the morning, A.T.C. I said goodbye there. The commander said nice words, and they gave me applause in the afternoon to the movies with Joan. In the evening I've been to the pub first, afterwards to the L.P. dance.

14th of December 1942

I've received a letter from the Ministry of Aviation. On my birthday, on the 16th of December, I must go to Kensington to join the army.

15th of December 1942

I've been at the diamond factory for the last time. One of my colleagues gave me chocolate. I've received 90 cigarettes from Bill, £ 3 from the diamond cutters, and £ 5 extra from my boss.

16th of December 1942

Today it's my birthday. I'm now 18 years. This morning a lot of people are going to say good day. This afternoon I've been to Kensington. First, they wanted to keep me there, but the lieutenant permitted me to go home because I've organised a little party tonight. There were 4 boys, 4 girls, Mr and Mrs Clarke, Mrs Bransom's sister, and Mr and Mrs Bransom. At 9:00 o'clock, the Mayor of Camberwell did come to say goodbye to me personally. From Mr and Mrs Bransom, I've got a pair of house shoes and a fountain pen for Christmas. From Phyllis, I've got a lighter. From Mr and Mrs Clarke I've got a nice tie and from Dick beautiful blue writing paper and postcards. The party ended at 11.35 p.m.

THE END OF THE CITIZEN LIFE UNTIL AFTER THE WAR
_____

MILITARY SERVICE
_____

17th of December 1942

At 9:15, I left the house. Also, I've made a will that, in case there will something happen to me, Mr Bransom takes the money from the bank and would give it to mama with all my clothes, etc. or to Fre when they should come to England, or else he should wait until after the war. When I left the house, Mrs Bransom stood on the doorstep and started to cry.

First, I went to the Air Service. From there, they sent me to Sutherland House. At 3:00, I already wore a soldier's suit. I must stay there for a couple of weeks. At 5:00 I've got off until midnight. I've been going immediately to my house. When Mrs Bransom came home, she was very shocked. She didn't expect me. In the evening, I've been to the Co-op for one hour. Then I've been going with Milly to Joan. At 10:10, I left again, back to Kensington. Everyone was amazed to see me in khaki.

18th of December 1942

First I had to clean the canteen in the morning. Then at 1:00, I had to be with the captain of the Air Force. After that, I had to report myself somewhere together with 5 other boys. In the evening, after

5.00 o'clock when I got off, I danced at the 'Hammersmith' dance. I brought a girl to the train. Her name was Irene.

19th of December 1942

The whole morning I was busy cleaning the rooms. I've asked permission to sleep at home because I could go home. In the afternoon I've been shopping with Mr and Mrs Bransom. In the evening, the Co-op. In the evening, I broke up with Joan, this time for good.

20th of December 1942, Sunday

This morning I played football in favour of Bromar. We lost. I've played halfback for the first time. Bromar 1 - Effrontery 6. This afternoon I've been to the movies. This evening I visited for a while my friends at L.P. dance. Then I went for a walk with Ann (twins). I was back in Kensington at 10:00.

21st of December 1942

In the morning, I had an exam for the R.A.F. I wasn't good enough in arithmetic. I've to learn better in the evening to the 'Hammersmith dance.

22nd of December 1942

I've been to the Hammersmith dance with one of the soldiers. We both met a French girl, Françoise. She is 18, and she's coming from Paris.

24th of December 1942

In the afternoon, I went home, and I had a weekend off until Sunday midnight. In the evening, Co-op. I've made a walk with Phyllis. After the dance, I brought Joan back home. Mr Bransom has become today 37 years.

25th of December 1942

Christmas. In the afternoon with the Benavente family, the Hyatt's with little Miona came to visit me. I received a letter and a postcard from Irene Catlin in the morning. In the letter, there was a nice wallet.

26th of December 1942

First, I peeled potatoes for 7 people. Then I went by bike to Streatham to thank Irene personally. Afterwards, I've been on my bike back home. In the afternoon I've been to the movies with Joan. After that, I went to the elderly people of Bransom and slept there.

27th of December 1942, Sunday

At 6:00 I left and was home again at 7.00 o'clock. At 9:30, I went back to Sutherland House. I didn't keep my date with that girl from the A.W.B. It's the first time that I didn't keep a date.

29th of December 1942

I have been to a little party in the hospital next to us. I met a nurse, Kathleen Collett. I've brought her back home after the dance.

31st of December 1942

Today I've been to OST. John's Wood for the first time. This evening I will keep watch until tomorrow.

1st of January 1943

In the afternoon I've been to the movies. In the evening I've been to the pub with Kathleen Collett. I've received a letter from Bill within the letter 10/-.[50p] for the New Year.

2nd of January 1943

Went home. In the afternoon to the movies, in the evening, the Co-op.

3rd of January 1943, Sunday

In the afternoon, I've been with June, Doris, and Eddie. I took June to my house. Afterwards, she has brought me to the train. I was back at12.00 o'clock.

4th of January 1943

This evening I've been dancing in the 'Hammersmith' with Kathleen. It wasn't bad, but we left there at 10.00.

5th of January 1943

Been dancing in the 'Hammersmith'. I've met Mary (25). Brought her back home.

6th of January 1943

I've been to the pub with Mary. Had a lovely evening.

8th of January 1943

The Navy has replaced me. I'm going to be a machine air gunner.

9th of January 1943

In the evening, the Co-op.

10th of January 1943, Sunday

In the afternoon I've been to the movies with Dick. In the evening, the L.P. dance. Brought Joan back home.

11th of January 1943

Today I've been officially transferred.

13th of January 1943

I got dressed today. Very nice in my sailor suit. Much better than khaki. I'm now a Sailor 2nd class., so it's already a much better position. 12 days off.

14th of January 1943

I've been to Post 27. A nice evening with the R.A.F. In the afternoon I've been to the movies.

15th of January 1943

I've been to Mrs O'Toole with Dick. he was with Marie, and I was with June. She was there also.

16th of January 1943

I received a Red Cross message from mama this morning. Fre is interned. I've been to the football in the afternoon. Millwall 0 - Tottenham 3. Afterwards, I've been to Mrs Benavente. In the evening I've been to the Co-op with Dick. After the dance, we've been eating a sausage roll. There was possible something in that roll, so one of my teeth had become loose. I've brought Joan back home.

18th of January 1943

First I've been to the dentist this morning with Joan. The dentist had to pull out a tooth. This afternoon I've been to the movies. In the evening, I walked around.

19th of January 1943

In the afternoon I've been to the movies. In the evening, the Co-op.

20th of January 1943

For the first time, I've been to work. This week I've to work 4 days, to earn some money. In the evening I've been to a Civil Defence dance. A fantastic band.

21st of January 1943

In the evening, the Co-op.

22nd of January 1943

Today is the last day of work. I've received 86.10.-[£4.30p]. In the evening, I went home with Bill. Stayed there until 9:15, and then I went to Joan. I stayed there until...

23rd of January 1943

1:10 this morning. I went to bed at 2:00. I've spent the late afternoon with Mrs Wyatt. In the evening, the Co-op. Brought Elsie (17) back home.

24th of January 1943, Sunday

In the morning I played football. Bromar 8 - Bermondsey 0. I scored two goals, 2 goals were made of my crosses, and 2 times my shots were against the bar. My best match ever. Our supporters congratulated me.

In the afternoon, I visited the Benavente family. In the evening, C.P. Stones. I've brought Joan back home.

25th of January 1943

My leave has finished today. I reported myself at the Headquarters. I've got an extension of my leave. While I was there, I asked to play football. Next Saturday, I can play for the first time in the first Navy team in Tooting. When I came home, there was a letter for me from Fre. She is now in Liebenau, Germany. She feels good and is healthy. Also, in the letter, there was a picture of her. In the afternoon, I've been to the Red Cross and to the Prisoners of War. Afterwards, to Covent Garden. In the evening I've been to the movies with Dick. After that, I went to Mrs O'Toole.

26th of January 1943

I've been in bed all day. In the evening, the Co-op. I've brought Joan back home.

27th of January 1943

I've been to the Opera this afternoon with Mrs Bransom. They should perform 'La Traviata', but they performed 'Madame Butterfly'. It was very nice. In the evening, I've done a bit of Morse code at the A.T.C.

28th of January 1943

In the afternoon I've been going to a reception on the birth of Princess Margret Franciska. The Queen was also there. Afterwards, I had a meal and some drinks with 3 sailors who were also there and later went to the Co-op. I've brought Alice (22) back home.

29th of January 1943

In the afternoon I've been to the movies. In the evening, I brought Violet (22) back home.

31st of January 1943, Sunday

In the afternoon I've been to the movies with Dick. In the evening, L.P. dance. When I came home, June was there. I never brought her home.

1st of February 1943

I've been going again to the Headquarters today. Again, I've got 12 days' leave. Afterwards, I had to go by train to Morpeth (Northumberland). This evening I met a certain Violet (23) at the Co-op.

2nd of February 1943

I visited Violet in the afternoon. Then I went to the Co-op. I've brought Joan back home, and we had a little fight.

3rd of February 1943

I've been to the movies with Violet. Afterwards, we went for a walk. At 5:00, I visited the Catlin family. I've had a meal there, and I've got an egg, the second one that I had today.

4th of February 1943

In the evening, the Co-op. I've brought Elsie (17) back home.

5th of February 1943

In the evening to St. Giles. I made an appointment with a girl to bring her home, but when I went outside, I missed her.

6th of February 1943

We didn't play football this afternoon because of the bad condition of the field. So, I've been watching Millwall 4 - Aldershot 1. A surprisingly win because Aldershot is a good team. In the evening, the Co-op. Mrs Wanfield (Peggy) was there. She was only a few days out of the hospital and wanted to see me again. Brought her back home.

7th of February 1943, Sunday

I went out with Bill Boutelje. First went to a kosher restaurant for a meal. Afterwards, we went to Finsbury Park. Then to the movies. We had something to eat there.

In the evening, we went to the house of the apprentice of Bill, and we stayed there for a while. Two girls were there, and both gave me a picture, so I added it to my picture collection.

8th of February 1943

In the evening I've been to the movies with Violet. Afterwards??

9th of February 1943

Went to the sister of Mrs Bransom and stayed there overnight.

10th of February 1943

This afternoon I've been going to the firm. I slipped and hurt my knee.

11th of February 1943

It's the birthday of Mrs Bransom. I've given her money and taken her out to the movies.

In the evening, Phyllis came to visit me, and I brought her back home.

12th of February 1943

I got a message this morning that I don't need to go to Morpeth yet. It has been postponed until the 19th of February. So now it's the 5th week of my leave. This afternoon I've been buying clothes for Fre with Mrs Bransom. I've spent £ 3.13.-[£3.65p]. In the evening to the Co-op.

13th of February 1943

To the football in the afternoon. Dulwich Hamlet 4 - Southall 1. It wasn't very interesting. In the evening, I've had a cup of tea with Doris and Ted, who live upstairs. Afterwards, I went with Ted to the pub. Then to the Co-op. I've brought Pamela (18) back home.

14th of February 1943, Sunday

I've been playing football in the morning. Bromar 0 - Dagenham 1. We barely lost. In the afternoon I've been to the wedding party of Doris and Eddie, 2 good friends of mine.

In the evening I've been in the pub from 7:00-10:00. I became drunk. A girl Violet, who was there, had to bring me home.

15th of February 1943

I've been to the movies this evening with Phyllis.

16th of February 1943

This afternoon I went to the movies with Penny, the sister of Joan, who is on leave. In the evening, we go to the Co-op. I've brought Pamela (18) home.

17th of February 1943

I've been out in the afternoon with my old friends Danny and Pieter, who are both on leave. In the evening, I go to the movies with Pamela (19). Afterwards, we had supper in a snack bar, and then I brought her back home.

First, I had made an appointment with Joan and Penny, but I cancelled that. Otherwise, I couldn't have done that. I've made a good excuse.

18th of February 1943

I've brought Danny to the train because he went to Leicester. This evening the Co-op with Pamela, and after the dance, I brought her home.

19th of February 1943

This evening I left London and arrived at...

20th of February 1943

5:45 this morning in Morpeth. I've been staying in the waiting room until 9 o'clock. I arrived in the army camp at 9:15. Breakfast at 9:45 and at 9:50, I had already an appointment with Irene (18) from the W.R.A.F. for this evening. I went to Morpeth in the evening. On the way back, we were with 12 people in a taxi.

21st of February 1943

This morning the lessons have started. On Tuesday, we have our day off. In the evening I've been to Morpeth. I've brought Edith back home.

22nd of February 1943

I've been to the dentist. This evening I've been in Morpeth with Irene. We've been walking back home.

24th of February 1943

This evening is a movie evening in the army camp. I will go there. In the coming period, I will not be going out much because I want to get good results for my exams. Irene is washing my white collars for me all the time, and that's, of course, not easy.

1st of March 1943

Today I received letters for the first time. Also, I've received 2 Red Cross messages, one from mama and 1 from Jaap Soesan. The message of mama was written by cousin Fre.

Tonight there was a dance in the camp.

2nd of March 1943

Today I have had a day off. And this afternoon, I've been going to Morpeth. At 9:00, I was already back in the camp. I didn't feel good because I'd been drinking too much tea.

3rd - 7th March 1943

I've been studying in my room all the time and copying my notes.

8th of March 1943

This morning we should have a flight for the first time, but because of the weather, it's postponed. In the evening I am going to Morpeth. I've lost a bet about a character. That will cost me 10/-. [50p]

9th of March 1943

This morning I've got a free ride to Morpeth. I've had my hair cut. In the late afternoon, I've been to Newcastle. I've been to the movies with 2 girls from the army camp. In the evening I've been to the 'Oxford' and went dancing there. I've met Iris Hinnen (23). Made an appointment for the following Monday. I left at 9:15. I had been waiting 45 minutes for the bus.

10th of March 1943

To Morpeth, went dancing.

11th of March 1943

I've made a flight this morning and in the afternoon. Got the result of my exam. I was the first of the Dutch boys with 84. Seven of the boys had less than 60.

12th of March 1943

Today again, I have flown twice. In the evening I've been to Morpeth. I've been dancing from 8.00 until 1.00. I came home at...

13th of March 1943

2:15 in the morning. In the evening I've been again to Morpeth. At 9:00 I went back to the camp by bus.

15th of March 1943

In the evening I'm going to Newcastle. Iris didn't come. In all probability, because there have been 3 air-raid alarms this week. At 10:00, I was lying in my bed already.

16th of March 1943

I've been to the Patterson family. I had a meal there and had to be back on time in the camp.

20th of March 1943

I went to the movies with Irene, in Morpeth.

22nd of March 1943

We've had our second exam this afternoon. I suppose I will have a good result. In the evening I've been to Newcastle. I spent de evening in a cafe with Opdorp and King.

23rd of March 1943

In the evening I've been to the movies with an English boy from the course. I've met Ettie (24). Made an appointment with her for next Tuesday. Then I've been going back to Morpeth by bus. When I came off the bus, I met 2 girls from the W.A.A.F. I've made an appointment with both. With one on Thursday and the other one on Friday. So, these are 3 appointments in about two hours.

24th of March 1943

We've got the results of our exam today. This time I had 79%. I'm hardly studying now, so the final exam will be less. However, 79% isn't bad at all.

25th of March 1943

I've been to the dentist this afternoon. He has drilled a few fillings and put temporary fillings in those teeth until I must come back. Anyway, he has whitened my teeth, because the colour of my teeth are not so nice anymore. I've been to the movies with that girl of the W.A.A.F., Elsie Cragg (21). Had to walk back to the camp.

26th of March 1943

I went dancing in Morpeth. There were another six boys of us. They had to drink there a glass of beer with the Mayor. I left at 1.15 and...

27th of March 1943

arrived at 2:15 in the billet. I've been to Morpeth in the evening together with Elsie.

28th of March 1943

I've been in the evening to Morpeth with Dick. Again I had to walk back to the camp.

29th of March 1943

This morning at 11:30, we made a flight. When we descended and came out of the plane, we got the message that two planes of ours had collided. All the men aboard were dead. Among them were 5 Dutch people, one Englishman, one Scottish man, and the pilots were one from New Zealand and one Polish man. I've made flights with both pilots. Two of the Dutch boys slept in the same room with me. So of the four of us, just Dick and I remain. It's terrible what has happened. One of the boys who slept in my room had been married just 6 weeks before, and his wife is here in Morpeth.

Late in the evening, I go to Newcastle. I've met there Jackie Ritmeester. He is on 'The Floris'. I didn't see him since he was gone to the army.

30th of March 1943

I've been visiting my friends here this morning. I had to go back early because I had to go to the dentist again. In the evening I am going out with Elsie. And again, I had to walk back to the camp.

1st of April 1943

I've been to the movies with Elsie in the evening. Again I had to walk back to the camp.

3rd of April 1943

Our boys were buried this afternoon. Also, the other men who crashed were buried. I had to help carry the coffin. Afterwards, a girl came to me and asked me if I was going somewhere. I've seen her once at a dance event. I told her that I didn't have plans to go somewhere, so she asked me to come with her to her house and eat something with her and her family. I was going with her. It was very nice. They have taken pictures of me, and I have taken pictures of the girl. A little bit later, we walked, and at 6:30, I was going back to the camp because I had an appointment with my girlfriend, Elsie. So I saw her at 8.45.

4th of April 1943, Sunday

In the evening, I had been with Elsie. It was her last evening with me because tomorrow she is going on leave. I've had my final exam the whole day today.

5th of April 1943

Again my final exam is the whole day today. It's all oral. I passed. In the evening I've been to Morpeth to postpone a date because I don't have a day off tomorrow. It's the last week, and that's why we must fly as much as possible

6th of April 1943

I flew this morning. We were lucky that we didn't crash. A little window next to the pilot touched the propeller, and a little piece fell off.

7th of April 1943

We had a little farewell party in Morpeth. We all put together 10/-.[50p] per man. Afterwards, we've been to dance all together and didn't pay at all. Maureen was also there, the girl with whom I had a meal after the funeral. After the dance, I walked with her for a short time to her house. Together with a few drunk officers, we woke the boys up in the billet and made a lot of noise.

8th of April 1943

I flew three times today. In the evening I've been to Morpeth and stayed in the evening with the Forman family.

9th of April 1943

I flew again 3 times today. The result of the final exam. I've got 72%, so that's good. In the evening I walked with Marjory.

10th of April 1943

We left in the evening at 9:55. I had tea late in the afternoon with the Forman family. Afterwards to the pub with Maureen, her brother Allon and his girlfriend. We took a glass of beer on my health. Thereafter, we had supper at the Forman family.

Maureen brought me to the train. I saw on her bag an air gunners' badge, which I didn't see before. So I said something about the badge, and she answered that if I didn't mind, she would wear it for me. She is already in love with me, but I see her as a friend, nothing more.

12th of April 1943

I left this morning at 8:45 to London by train. Arrived in London at 11:40. Went to the doctor in the afternoon because my throat is painful. Afterwards, I've been to the movies. When I came back home, there was Phyllis and my friend Dick welcomed me.

13th of April 1943

In the evening to the Co-op. I stayed in bed the whole day.

14th of April 1943

Have been to Niena Wyatt, the sister of Mrs Bransom. There were 5 women with 5 babies. I've been to the movies with Phyllis.

15th of April 1943

To the Co-op in the evening. The minute I saw her (no doubt, Joan), I was on. I've tried to forget her but until this moment I can't. I talked with her, and we did drink something. In the end, I brought her back home.

16th of April 1943

I've made a walk with Joan to Greenwich Park this afternoon. Beautiful weather, and we talked about the past. She is not working now because within two weeks she is going to the W.A.A.F.

I've received this morning a letter from Elsie, who I dated in Morpeth.

17th of April 1943

I received a letter from Elsie again. I left London by train at 3:40 this afternoon and arrived at around 8.00 at the camp.

20th of April 1943

I've asked a girl working in the Naafi to come with me for a walk. She is old and ugly (29) but very helpful. I get from her chocolate and cigarettes without vouchers. I received a nice picture from Elsie.

21st of April 1943

I've been walking again with Muriel. It's the name of that girl from the Naafi.

24th of April 1943

Yesterday evening there was a dance evening of the W.A.A.F. It was fantastic. There were also girls from an A.T.B. camp in this neighbourhood because there are not enough girls in our camp. Of course, I've met a girl, Joan (18, A.T.B.).

I had a wonderful evening. Otherwise, the camp is boring.

25th of April 1943, Sunday

We arrived with the 12 of us in West Rainham. We will get here a special course about gunnery for 14 days.

26th of April 1943

In the evening I've been dancing in the gymnasium. I've brought Corporal Cobb (22) to the billet.

27th of April 1943

I've given the corporal two collars to wash for me. In the evening I've made a walk.

12th of May 1942

To the movies with Violet.

13th of May 1942

Today it was 2 years ago that I left Belgium. Co-op.

14th of May 1942

Coöp and A.F.S.

15th of May 1942

Went with my friend Johnny to the Co-op. I've brought home Winnie (19) and Nellie. We came home late, and then Johnny slept here.

This morning I got a letter from mama, which was forwarded by the Zomerplaag family. Somebody who came here brought it for me. There were also 2 pictures. I will have them enlarged. Also, I've bought a second-hand bike from Mr Russell, who lives downstairs. It cost me £ 5.10.-.[£5.50p]

16th of May 1942

In the morning, I tried it on for the first time my suit. I've been sending Red Cross letters to mama, to the Muller's from the Leyerplein and the Verduin family from the Ruysch street.

In the afternoon to the movies with Violet (21). In the evening, the Co-op

17th of May 1942, Sunday

I've been the whole day with Mr and Mrs Bransom to Sutton, to very close friends of ours. We came back home at 8.00. Afterwards, I've been to the L.P. dance for half an hour. I've won two free tickets for Monday evening in the Spot Waltz. I've brought Joan (20) home.

19th of May 1942

For the first time I've made a tour around S.E. London, or in other words a few cities.

20th of May 1942

To the movies with Johnny. Today there was a meeting about the diamond trade.

22nd of May 1942

Today it's 2 years ago that in the evening, I left Le Havre with the ship to come to England.

23rd of May 1942

Two years ago I arrived in England. In the evening, I broke up after seven days. Afterwards, the Co-op.

24th of May 1942

In the afternoon we were driving for half an hour, in the rain. In the evening, the Co-op. I've brought Joan back home.

25th of May 1942 Sunday (now dating Joan).

Covent Garden Opera House with Joan. Afterwards, we drank tea at our house, after that L.P. dance. Brought Joan home.

https://www.nationalww2museum.org/visit/museum-campus/us-freedom-pavilion/warbirds/north-american-b-25-mitchell

https://www.boeing.com/history/products/b-25-mitchell.page

https://dunsfoldairfield.org/raf-1943-1944/

14th of May 1943

I've been to Norwich in the evening with one of our boys, Louis Dekker. I've met Dawn Dust. Had a lovely evening. I had a meal in the Princess restaurant.

16th of May 1943, Sunday

I've made a ride with an English boy. We went to Dereham, that's the same distance from our camp as Norwich. It's just a little village. We had a meal in a nice hotel, the best and only one there. We laughed because the waitress fought with her boss.

19th of May 1943

In one week, I've flown 16.20. Beautiful weather and it's fantastic in the air. In the evening, I went for a ride with Joan (21), one from the Officer's lesson.

20th of May 1943

I went out with Joan. Also with us are her friend Mary (18) and a boy Titch. The four of us went for a ride. Came back after midnight.

21st of May 1943

This morning I washed my clothes. This afternoon I left. The weather is perfect. I hope it will stay like this during my leave. Tomorrow my girlfriend Elsie from Morpeth, number 1, will most likely spend the weekend with us because she is stationed in Uxbridge. At 4.00 o'clock I went for my leave. I've got a free ride to Norwich. Went to the movies, had a good meal and then to the pub. I've slept in the Y.M.C.A.

22nd of May 1943

In the morning I've been to London. In the afternoon, I've picked up Elsie in Uxbridge. In the evening, we've been dancing in the Co-op. Elsie stayed with us overnight.

23rd of May 1943, Sunday

I'm 3 years in England today. In the afternoon I've been to the movies with Elsie. Then to the city... we had a meal at Folman's, afterwards to the pub, then to a dance where they tried to rip me off. They didn't get the chance. They gave me the money back.

24th of May 1943

In the afternoon, I had pictures taken. Afterwards, I've been to the firm. I've received 8.2[£4.10p]-. from the boss. Went out with the Davis family, Bill. First, we went to eat at Folman's, afterwards to the show "It's foolish, but it is fun". Very good. After that, I've been to Lyons with Bill and Ronnie Davies. I met June (23) in the subway and brought her home.

25th of May 1943

I've been to the movies in the afternoon together with Mrs Mien, the sister of Mrs Bransom who lives now in our house. In the evening to the Co-op, afterwards to the Milk bar with Jean (30).

26th of May 1943

I've visited the Brown family. After that, I visited Mrs Benavente. I stayed there and ate something. Then I met Elsie. I've been to the pub and afterwards to the Covent Garden Dancing. Elsie left at 10:00.

29th of May 1943

I've received this morning 4 letters. At 6:00, I woke up already and started to read them. One was a postcard from Fre from Germany. She wrote that she's speaking good English now, which may come in handy.

I've lost my battle dress, and that's not funny. If you are here on leave, you always have lost something when you return. In the evening I've been to a dance in this neighbourhood. I've never had an experience like this. It was in a cabin. There was no electric light but a gaslight which stood in the middle of the hall. Nearly every 5 minutes, it went out, and someone had to stand on a chair to pump up the gas. It's the most impossible that I've experienced. I will never go back there. There were more than 200 people, and there was only room for about 50 people. It looks like a sardine can.

30th of May 1943, Sunday

I've almost nothing to report. In the evening, I was in the cabin when a girl with long hair drove along. She stopped when I looked through the window, and we've talked for a while. Later I brought her to the farm where she was working.

31st of May 1943

I've been to Norwich by bike. Later I loaned my bike to an English boy from the camp. I missed the bus to the camp. So I had to walk all the way back. It was because of a girl who showed us the road but, by purpose, made a detour. At...

1st of June 1943

...3.00 o'clock I went finally to bed.

3rd of June 1943

I've been to a dance in Ringway. I met Dorothy (33).

5th of June 1943

I've been to Norwich with four of our boys. Went to the pub for a drink.

9th of June 1943

I've been to Norwich with Connie (22). Went to the movies.

10th of June 1943

I've made a bike ride with Margaret (25) from the infirmary.

11th of June 1943

I've been to Norwich. I've been drinking too much. I missed the bus, and it was my own fault. So I had to walk. Just outside Norwich, I went to sleep in the field.

12th of June 1943

At 5:45, I woke up. I started to walk. Later I was picked up by someone from the post office, and I could come with him a big part of the journey in his car. I was back in the camp at 7.30. I almost had to stand for a parade, but I got rid of it with an excuse. I've been to Norwich in the evening with Penny the sister of Joan, who is stationed here in the neighbourhood. First, we had something to eat in Curat House, afterwards, we went dancing in Sampson. It was a nice evening.

29th of April 1943

I flew today for the first time in Ventura. In the evening I've been walking again with my little corporal. I've got my collars back, and so I'm free again.

30th of April 1943

I've been to the W.A.A.F. dance in the evening with Violet. I've become friends with a boy who is also flying here, Ted and with his wife, Dorothy. We had a lovely evening.

1st of May 1943

Today I have a day off. I've been to Fakenham. First I eat something and afterwards go to the movies. After that I made a walk, then I ate again and had a drink until I went to meet Ted and his wife. We drank a glass of beer and then we went dancing. We had fish and chips. After dancing, I've met a W.A.A.F. corporal, Edith, I should bring her to the billet in the camp, but I didn't see her at the gate. It doesn't matter.

2nd of May 1943 Sunday

The weather was good today. Tonight at 7:00 I must meet Violet.

3rd of May

I've been to a show in the evening, compiled with large crews of the R.A.F., men and women. It was fantastic, better than some shows in London. It's already over with Violet, and I've brought Vera (28) back home.

4th May 1943

I've been dancing at the Naafi in the evening. It was very nice.

5th May 1943

I've been to Fakenham, have been to a dance which was organised by the camp after a football match whereby the R.A.F. team of our station defeated a team of the Army 6-1. I also have met two of the best players, here in England and in Scotland. Alf Kirchen from Arsenal and Jimmy Dodds from Scotland. Had a nice time dancing.

6th May 1943

I've been to an ENSA show in the camp. I've brought Gwen (22) to the billet

7th May 1943

Because I was bored, I've been to the movies.

8th May 1943

I've been to Fakenham in the afternoon. During the dancing, I met Rose Streetin in the evening. She is 22. Brought her to the billet when we came back. Always when I meet a lovely girl, it's on the last evening. Tomorrow we leave.

9th May 1943 Sunday

At 3.00 o'clock in the afternoon, I went back to Attlebridge. This morning I received a picture from Rose.

16th June 1943

I've been to Norwich. Had a meal in the Princess restaurant. After that, I went dancing. I've met there one of the best dancers, Ellen Walker (19). She is really a great dancer. Made an appointment for next Friday. I've got a message from Fre today. Mama has been interned.

17th June 1943

In the evening, I went for a ride with Margaret (25) from the infirmary.

18th June 1943

I've been to Norwich, but first I went to Curat House to eat something. I've met the boss of the business, a Jewish man, Mr. Levy.

Afterwards, I went dancing with Eileen. She is much better than Joan. I had a wonderful evening. I've brought Eileen back home, and I've been sleeping at the Y.M.C.A.

19th June 1943

Today it was eight years ago that my late father passed away. I went to London because I've got 40 hours on leave. I've met Joan, and together we have visited friends who I haven't seen for a long time. Joan was also on 40 hours' leave.

20th June 1943

This morning I've taken the baby of Mrs. Bransom, little Rita, to Joan's house. This afternoon, just before I went back to Norwich, little Rita said to Sal. I was so happy with it. She is 22 months now. Phyllis, who still is my loyal girlfriend, brought me to the train.

26th June 1943

I've been out with Connie (21), her friend Jackie and Louis Dekker. We went to Norwich.

While driving my bike fast, before we went to the train, I got stuck with my ear on the barbed wire. My ear was bleeding a lot. From Norwich again, we went by train to Attlebridge station. From there by bike to the camp. On the way, the police stopped us, and I received a fine for the first time in my life. I didn't have a light on my bike. That was the reason that I received this fine.

27th June 1943 Sunday

I drove with Louis Dekker to Foulsham. Connie and Jackie are stationed there. However, we haven't seen them.

30th June 1943

I've been to Norwich with my telegraphist, Jan de Jong. Had a meal at Curat House. Afterwards, we went dancing in the 'Sampson.' Eileen was also there. Made an appointment for tomorrow, Thursday. She had brought us to the bus.

1st July 1943

I went to Norwich at 4.00 o'clock in the afternoon. Again I am on leave. If you are flying personnel, you get every five weeks' leave.

This time I won't go to London, but I will go to Nottingham... I have seen there the manager of our Naafi on our camp, and we have been drinking a cup of coffee. Afterwards, I had a meal. After that I drank something with a few American soldiers. after that I met Eileen, and together we went dancing in the 'Sampson.'

3rd July 1943

Went to the city in the afternoon together with Bill, Margaret, and the little daughter of Bill, Margaret. First, we ate in the Ritz, and afterwards, we went to the movies upstairs. I've paid for everything.

4th of July 1943 Sunday

In the afternoon, I went to Elsie Cragg (21). We broke up a short time ago because of Margaret. I stayed at Elsie's house for a cup of tea. Also, I got their supper and stayed until 10.00 o'clock. I had an appointment with Margaret to go with her to the movies. So I had to leave her waiting for me. When I came home, she was very angry. That girl wants to go out with me every evening, but I will be damned if I do it. She took and hid my pyjamas out of anger, and so I, for the time of my leave I, had to sleep without my pyjamas.

5th July 1943

In the morning I've been to the city to do some shopping. Afterwards, I've been to Elsie and had lunch there. In the afternoon I've been with her to the city, and we went to a nice show. Vera Lynn was there on stage. In the evening we went to a pub and drunk there a couple of glasses of beer. Elsie went home at 9.00 o'clock because she wanted to see a friend of hers who was on leave. So I've been to the dance on my own. From the dance, I've brought a girl back home, Doris (21). Afterwards, I went to the place where I had rented a room, but before I arrived there, I met another girl, Evelyn, and stayed with her until 2.00 o'clock. I was pretty drunk.

6th July 1943

At 10.00 in the morning, I came out of my bed and went back by bus to Arnold, where I stayed, had a meal, shaved, and then went back to the city. I've been dancing with Elsie and a friend of hers. Went to the movies in the evening with Margaret. Went to bed at 10.00 o'clock.

7th July 1943

Went dancing in the Palais in the afternoon. I've met corporal Pat Malone, (23), (W.A.A.F.). A nice girl. She was in plain clothes. Yesterday she was also there, while I was with Elsie. I didn't pay attention to her because she was in uniform, but she smiled very friendly. I danced with her the whole afternoon. In the evening I went dancing again at the same place, and she was there too with her friend. After the dance, we went to the Y.M.C.A. to get something to eat and afterwards they walked for a little time with me. I will write her a letter because tomorrow I must go back to Attlebridge. Again my leave is over.

8th July 1943

Woke up at 5.00 o'clock. Left for London and arrived there at 11.30. Visited Joan for a while because she also was on leave. By train to Norwich in the afternoon. Mrs. Bransom and little Rita brought me to the train. The first thing in Norwich was taking a meal in the Curat House. Afterwards, I've been dancing in Sampson. Eileen, my partner, was there also but with somebody else. She didn't know I came to Norwich. The boy had to go at 10.00 o'clock and then Eileen came to sit with me. I was too tired to dance. I brought Eileen a little way to her house after the dance, and the three of us took a taxi and let us drive to the camp.

10th July 1943

Have been to Norwich. Went to the Sampson and met Eileen there.

12th July 1943

Got a message from Fre with a picture, but she didn't write the letter herself.

15th July 1943

There was a good show at the camp. I liked it very much.

16th July 1943

I hitchhiked to Norwich. Had eaten with my telegraphist in Curat House. Then I've gone to the movies with Eileen. Walkedto her home. Afterwards, I bought some chips. Then by bus back to the camp.

18th July 1943 Sunday

Nothing to report.

19th July 1943

I've been to a movie show in the camp. 'Crossroads'. A nice film.

21st July 1943

In the evening I went to Norwich. Went dancing in the Sampson. Eileen brought me to the bus. Jan Schriver's, my pilot, stood on one side of the bus with a W.A.A.F. girl. Me, the air gunner on the other side.

23rd July 1943

I've been to the dance in the camp. Didn't dance. Met a new W.A.A.F. girl, Sybil. Brought her afterwards to the billet.

24th July 1943

I've been to Norwich. Had a nice meal. After that, I have been drinking a glass of beer with a sergeant of the air camp. Then to the Sampson. Eileen brought me to the bus. Made an appointment with Barbara (22). She is working for the Church Army Canteen. Every day they come to our camp with tea, cakes and all whatthat we need there.

25th July 1943 Sunday

I've been walking in the evening with Sybil (22).

26th July 1943

I've got a message from Fre today. The best letter that I have received, she has received all the clothes that I sendsent her in February. Mother is interned in Amersfoort. Fre is hoping that mama will be with her in her camp. Gladys Borst, a friend of Fre in the camp, has sent me a postcard too.

27th July 1943

I've flown very late today. For the first time, I've been on a half operation flight this afternoon. At 6.15 we flew, 'air-sea rescue'. We had found three Americans on the sea. Later they were rescued by a boat that had the task of picking up people after they fell into the sea. I made a little mistake; it will cost me my crew and my promotion.

29th July 1943

Have been to a show at the camp.

1st August 1943

I've been going to Ringland in the evening for half an hour. With some of our boys. Pub.

2nd August 1943

I've been to Honingham. Half an hour walk. There was a dance in a little cabin. Met a girl, a W.A.A.F. in plainclothes, who was on leave. Her rank was a sergeant. Dorothy (23). Before the end of the dance, I walked a little bit.

3rd August 1943

I'm no longer in the Schrijver crew. I went to my Gunnery Leader. He will talk about me with the Commander. Maybe I will not be longer an air gunner, he said.

4th August 1943

I had to come on roll call because I didn't let me report on Monday evening. The 1st Officer had seen me. Tomorrow I will get the result. I've made a date in Norwich with Doris Spurrell (20).

5th August 1943

I had to go to the Commander, but I was not punished. I only have had a warning because it was the first time.

7th August 1943

To dance in the Concert Hall. I've brought Gwen (31) to the billet.

8th August 1943 Sunday

I've been to Norwich. Eileen brought me to the bus.

9th August 1943

I've been walking with Gwen (31).

10th August 1943

Today I've been on leave again. I had a nice meal. Went dancing with Doris. Before, I walked into a pub because I was thirsty. I meet Mr. Brown there, the man who hired me in 1940 at Monro in Covent Garden. I've brought Doris back home after the dance. Then I went back to the Y.M.C.A. I arrived at 11.57.

11th August 1943

I've been to London in the morning. To the movies in the afternoon. To a show with Phyllis in the evening. Have a nice day.

12th August 1943

I've been visiting the Benavente family. And the Catlin family. In the afternoon I went dancing in the Locarno. Had tea with the Catlins. In the evening, the Co-op. In between to the pub with Pamela. At...

13th August 1943

...1.15 I came back home because I had a discussion with two other boys about politics. Afterwards, I brought Pamela to her house. In the morning, I went to the firm. The boss asked me if I would come to work there. I've refused. I've received from him £2.-.-. From Bill I received £1.-.-. and from the boys £1.10.-[£1.50p]. Afterwards, I met Miss Lee Hawton.

14th August 1943

I've met Doris from Norwich, who came to London together with her mother and sisters. We went all together to Walthamstow, to the future husband of one of the sisters. In the afternoon, all of us went to Waterloo Station to meet our brother of Doris, who came on leave. Afterwards, Doris and I went to the movies. Then we had a meal at Lyons. Later I brought Doris to Walthamstow. On my way back, I've taken a trolley bus and three taxis. And then I arrived in Liverpool Street. From there, I had to walk all the way to Camberwell. The weather was good. Full moon.

15th August 1943 Sunday

I went out with Bill Boutelje, Ronnie, the boy in which house he lives, another two boys and two girls who all live in the neighbourhood. We've been to Windsor. Had a lovely day.

16th August 1943

Together with Irene Catlin, I've picked up Jimmy from the camp because he should come to London. However, he didn't come. (I had a little accident). The two of us went to Folman's to eat something. Then we went to Richmond by bus. At 6.00 o'clock we went back to the city by bus and had a lovely meal at Lyons. Then we are going to Covent Garden Dance Hall for dancing. They did formation dancing there. Went back home by tram.

17th August 1943

Yesterday I received a tax assessment. I still must pay £ 8.7.9[£8.40p]. I will go there tomorrow. Today I've said goodbye to the Benavente family. In the evening, E. & C. dance. I've brought Venus (22) back home.

18th August 1943

First, I've been to the Income-tax office. I've told them that I should pay after the war. I've brought my bike away because if I go back after my leave, I will take my bike to the camp. This afternoon I had to go back to the camp. Mrs. Bransom and little Rita, her sister Miena and her baby have brought me to the train. On the train I met an American, his name was Herman. When we arrived in Norwich, he helped me with my suitcase, while I was busy with my bike. Together we went for a meal at the American Red Cross. I left there my suitcase and my bike. At 9.30 o'clock I've brought my suitcase to the bus, and a friend of mine took it to the camp. Later I went by bike to the camp.

19th August 1943

Today it's Fre's birthday, and I wish her all the best and hope that she will soon be together with mama and that the three of us can be together again. She is 21 years now, a grownup woman. I've received a letter from her who arrived at the camp during my leave.

20th August 1943

Because the bus isn't working, I've been to the dance at the camp this evening. I had an appointment with Doris, so I've cancelled the date by phone. Then I sent her a telegram. I got a date into the bargain with the operator on the other side of the line. Her name is Muriel Mallet (18). This is a 'blind date'.

21st August 1943

I've been to Norwich by bike. I've been dancing with Doris in the Sampson. First, we had to wait for half an hour in the queue. It was so crowded that we went home already at 10.00 o'clock. We had taken home chips, made them warm there, and together with her mother, we had a nice meal. I left there at 11.50.

24th August 1943

I've been to Norwich by bike for a foxtrot competition. Eileen, who should have come and danced with me, didn't come. So I went back to the camp because we had there a big dance event since we will leave here next week. I've met Nancy (22). I brought her after the dance to the bus, which brought them back to their own camp.

25th August 1943

It should be today, the birthday of my late father. He should become now 48 years. I've got a message from Fre. Maybe mama is in France now.

27th August 1943

Together with three of my friends I've been to Norwich. First, we had a meal at Curat House. We laughed tremendously. Afterwards, I've been to a show in the Hippodrome with Doris. Lew Stone and his band were playing there. It was fantastic. In his band were a blind pianist and a very good trumpet player with just one arm. The pianist had a very nice voice. An old friend of mine also played in the band, Teddy Watmore, who had his own band in the Loughborough Hotel. At 10.00 I was in a hurry to catch the bus, and so I hadn't any time to stay with Doris.

28th August 1943

I've been to Drayton for dancing. I've been walking with Iris (18). A very nice girl. Had a nice evening at a little dance there.

29th August 1943 Sunday

Went for an hour to the Five Ringers. I was drinking a couple of beers with one of the boys, Joop Velleman.

30th August 1943

I've been transferred with the whole squadron. We travelled the whole day. We didn't even know where we were going.

31st August 1943

Queens day. We all received 50 cigarettes and 2/-[10p]. Worked very hard today to get all the stuff out of the station.

1st September 1943

I've been to the Lasham pub to drink a beer. I've met Ruby (22). Brought her to the billet.

2nd September 1943

I spent the evening in the Naafi with Ruby. Afterwards, I brought her to the billet.

3rd September 1943

I didn't wait for Ruby. I went to the New Inn pub. I met Iris (22). She is in the land army. After closing, I've brought her home.

6th September 1943

I've been to London because there was something about Fre that I had to discuss. The Consulate of South Africa had asked me to pay £27.13.5 [£27.63p]. Because they had sent money to Fre while she was still in Holland. I've told them that I should pay this after the war.

At 6.00 o'clock I was back in Alton. Iris was waiting for me on the train, and we went to the movies.

8th September 1943

I've been to an R.A.F. dance at the camp with Iris and her friend Jean. There was an Englishman who danced the whole evening with Iris, so I let her, and this is finished.

9th September 1943

This afternoon I received a message from Fre. She has sent a picture also. In the evening, I've been to an ENSA show in the camp with Ena (20).

10th September 1943

I've been to the New Inn. Ena had come too with two friends. She didn't feel well, and I have brought her back to the billet.

11th September 1943

I've been to Alton with two Jewish boys from the R.A.F. We've been dancing. Barbara (25) walked with me for a while. She invited me to her wedding, if that will be while we are still here.

12th September 1943 Sunday

I've been to the New Inn in the evening. It was boring. On my way to home, I've met a W.A.A.F. girl, and I've brought her to the billet. Olive Baguley (25).

14th September 1943

I've been to the movies in Alton with Olive. It was a nice evening. A nice girl. I will stay with her for the coming time.

16th September 1943

I've been to Alton with Olive. Went to the movies and afterwards, we had a meal in the W.V.S. canteen.

17th September 1943

I've been to London in the evening. Have danced in the E & C.

18th September 1943

In the morning, I've been to West End to get an address of a Rabbi who could lead the services on the coming Jewish Holidays. In the afternoon, I have visited Joan. She, too, had a leave of 24 hours. I've brought her with her friend to the train. At 8.30 I travelled back to Alton.

19th September 1943 Sunday

Nothing to report.

21st September 1943

Went to the movies in the camp. Received today a message from Fre.

24th September 1943

I'm going to Alton tonight, dancing. I met Sis (18). She walked along with me for a while. Have a date with her for tomorrow evening. There will be a nice dance with a good band.

25th September 1943

Went to Alton and met Sis there. We went dancing, 5/-[25p]. However, I couldn't pay for her. It's the first time that I didn't pay for a girl.

26th September 1943

For the first time, I went for a walk with Paula.

27th September 1943

I received a message from Fre this morning. From her friend Gladys too. I went out with Paula. ?

28th September 1943

I've got on leave for 48 hours. Dick Koning went with me to London. In the evening to the Co-op. There were five girls who I'd dated with in earlier days. At 11.00 o'clock, I said good night to Milly. Went for a meal with Pam and Dick first, then to the Milk bar. Then the two of us brought Pam home.

29th September 1943

First, in the morning, Dick and I visited June Morse, my earlier date (1941). In the afternoon, I went to the firm. I received £4.16.- [£4.80p]. From the people there. Afterwards went to the movies with Dick. Then we had a meal in Lyons Corner House, and then we went back home quickly. Phyllis was at our home. I brought Dick to the train. Then I had a lovely evening at Bill Boutelje and the Davis family.

30th September 1943

Today it's Yom Tov New year. I hope this year will be more successful than the last. I hope that all the families will be reunited very soon. I went to Aldershot to be at the synagogue service for soldiers who are in the army. Afterwards, we've got a lovely kosher meal. We had to march off neatly, and because I was the only one in a sailor uniform among 300 soldiers and 4 R.A.F. boys, I got the honour of leading the parade.

In the afternoon, I went to the movies with de R.A.F. boys, who are also from the camp. 'The Man in Grey'. A fantastic film. Afterwards, we had a meal, and then we travelled back to the camp.

1st October 1943

In the evening to the Naafi with Olive. She just came back from leave. Brought her to the billet.

2nd October 1943

I've received three messages from Germany. Two from Gladys, the friend of Fre, and one from Fre. This evening I will go with Olive to an ENSA show in the camp.

3rd October 1943 Sunday

To the New Inn with Olive.

6th October 1943

In the evening, I went on leave. When I arrived at home, there were Joan and Phyllis welcomed me. Brought Joan back home.

7th October 1943

I went to the factory to tell them that I was coming to work for four days. Afterwards, I've seen a nice movie. 'Stage Door Canteen'. There were six bands in this film.

In the evening, Co-op. Brought Joan back home.

8th October 1943

I've been to St. Giles. I met there my old friend Johnny. It was an awful evening. Almost nobody was there. The first day today that I've been working. I made nothing. What I've made was good.

9th October 1943

Today it's Yom Kippur. I fasted today. In the morning, I've been to the synagogue. At 1.00 o'clock I met Bill, and we went to the football. Tottenham 2 - Brighton 0. It was not a good match. In the evening, I had a Yom Tov meal with the Davis family. Stayed there the whole evening.

10th October 1943 Sunday

It's Rita Bransom's birthday today. She turned two years old. In the morning, I've taken her for a visit to Phyllis and her mother. In the afternoon I played football. Weights 5 - Bromar 1.

I played well but wasn't lucky. I was very tired. My friend Dick came to our house. Together we went dancing with Thelma (22) in Loughborough in the evening. Brought Thelma back home. Made an appointment for coming Wednesday.

11th October 1943

After work, I went to the Palladium with Bill, KURT, and Ronnie Davis. A very good show. Max Miller, Ann Shelton, Issy Bonn, and Billy Cotton and his band. Then we had a meal. Afterwards, we went to the Covent Garden dance hall for about 20 minutes.

12th October 1943

In the evening I've been to the movies with my friend Dick. Two nice films. 'Watch on the Rhine' and 'Crazy to Kill'. Afterwards, to the Milk bar.

13th October 1943

Today I've worked for the last time. I didn't keep the date with Thelma (22). Instead, I went to the 'Regal' dance hall on Marble Arch. I met Marie Westhead (20). She is a W.R.E.N. A lovely girl. I will write her regularly. First, I brought her and her friend to the Subway. Then I had a meal in Lyons Corner House.

14th October 1943

In the afternoon, I said goodbye to the Benavente family. Then I've been dancing in the Locarno. Met Ella (19) there. Oslo is a very handsome girl. Made a date with her for my next leave. At 6.00 o'clock in the evening, I went to a show with Dick and Mr. and Mrs. Bransom. But it wasn't nice at all. Then I went home, took all my things, and went to the train. I missed the train, one minute too late, and had to wait 1 hour and 10 minutes for the next one.

15th October 1943

I've been dancing in Alton in the evening. Brought Joan back home. It was a very good band.

17th October 1943

This morning I've been put on roll call because I didn't do what they told me to do. Other boys from my cabin too. Tomorrow we'll get the result in the evening to Naafi with Olive.

Had to come to the Commander. I only got a warning. The other two boys got two days hard. I had to bring them food as a punishment. So I got off well. This afternoon I received a letter and a picture from Marie Westhead. In the evening to the Naafi with Jimmy and Dick. Brought Olive to the billet.

19th October 1943

Yesterday evening when I went to the Naafi, my bike had disappeared suddenly. I immediately had a suspicion. When that boy came back I asked him if he had taken my bike, he gave me a big mouth and lied to me.

20th October 1943

I had reported the case, and so he had to go to the Commander. He didn't get punished because of my report but because he went out of the camp without permission. Earlier, he had taken and wore my good trousers at Attlebridge. Then I told him that if he ever should take something from me without asking, I should report him.

In the evening I went to the Naafi dance. Brought Olive back to the billet.

21st October 1943

Went with Olive this evening to an ENSA show in the camp.

23rd October 1943

I woke up this morning at 5.00 o'clock. We departed to West Raynham for 14 days. I was there also last April. We arrived this afternoon at 2.00 o'clock. I had a girl here, Rose Streetin, she is transferred to a camp here nearby, so I called her immediately.

In the evening, she came by truck. This truck is driving every evening. I went with Rose to the movies here in the camp. They have a beautiful cinema. At 9.30, I brought Rose back to the truck.

24th October 1943 Sunday

The course started today. Rose came again, and again we went to the cinema. A nice film. At 9.30, I brought her again to the truck. Afterwards, I've brought another W.A.A.F., I even don't know her name, to the cabin.

25th October 1943

I've been to Fakenham Met Rose there. We ate egg and chips. We danced for half an hour. The both of us had to go back by bus at 10.00 o'clock.

26th October 1943

Dance in the camp. Rose couldn't come because it was domestic night. I didn't like it. Only the band was good. Received the message that our Commander had been shot.

27th October 1943

Rose came again here to the camp. Then to the movies. Nothing else to do. The camp is not as nice as it was when I came here for the first time.

30th October 1943

This afternoon I've been dancing with Eileen in the 'Sampson'. After that we drank a cup of tea, then I went to the house of Doris. With her, I went to the movies. After that, we had supper. Doris brought me to the train. Before I went this afternoon to the 'Sampson', I first went with some American soldiers to the museum. It was very interesting.

31st October 1943

Nothing important to report. Rose didn't come to the camp; she missed the truck.

1st November 1943

Went with Rose to the movies here in the camp.

2nd November 1943

I've had a few different exams today. It went well. This evening I'm studying guns (machine guns). My friend, Albert Apeldoorn is killed. Het is fallen above Cherbourg. He got married just three months ago.

3rd November 1943

This evening I've been to the movies with Rose. For the first time in the past five weeks, I've flown today. Received two messages from mama.

4th November 1943

I've been to a dance with Rose in the camp. Didn't have a good evening.

6th November 1943

I've been to Fakenham to dance. I've met Ena (20), a land army girl. The dance was very crowded. Also, we have eaten eggs and chips.

7th November 1943 Sunday

Rose didn't come. Went all by myself to the cinema in the camp. Joan Hearn is 22 today.

8th November 1943

I've been to Fakenham with Maurice Goudeketting, a Jewish boy. He has come to the squadron a short time ago. Then we ate egg and chips with Ena and her friend. The girls didn't like eggs because they eat them so often, so we got 2.

9th November 1943

This morning at 8.00 o'clock we left from West Rainham back to Lasham. There was a postcard from a friend of Fre in Germany, Gladys Borst.

I've heard that I will be placed in a new crew at Off. VI.II. Stein. To the Naafi. I brought Olive to the billet, and she was happy that I was back.

10th November 1943

Today 7 months ago, I became an air gunner. Naafi. Brought Olive to the billet.

11th November 1943

Day of the Ceasefire. Cafe Continental in the Naafi. Brought Olive to the billet.

14th November 1943 Sunday

I've been to Alton with Dick Koning, Teddie Aartsen and Joop Velleman. We had a meal there, but we laughed there more than we did eat. At 10.30 we went back to the camp. Very cold. My W.R.E.N. has been very ill.

15th November 1943

Nothing to report today.

16th November 1943

In the morning I've been to London. I studied on the train. Tomorrow I've to do an exam to become a corporal. Came home at 1.00 o'clock, in the afternoon, to the movies with June (18). In the evening, I took her to my home. Stayed at home until 9.30 p.m. Then I left and took the last train to Alton. I didn't know that the bus from the station was going back to Alton at 11.00 o'clock. So I had to walk all the way. First I went to the police station, I couldn't sleep there either, in the street it was also impossible, then at...

17th November 1943

...2.15 this morning I started to walk and arrived at the camp at 4.00 o'clock. Had a dance.

18th November 1943

My exam is postponed until tomorrow. In the evening, the R.A.F. Dance Band no. 1 did come to the camp and has played in the concert hall. It was great. Brought Olive to the billet.

19th November 1943

I've had my exam and passed it. In the evening, the ENSA show wasn't nice at all, bringing Olive to the billet.

20th November 1943

The A.T.C. has given a show in the camp. Brought Olive to the billet.

21st 1943 Sunday

Nothing to report. Naafi.

23rd November 1943

In the evening to the cinema with Olive.

24th November 1943

In the evening, I dance in the Naafi. I talked the whole evening with my new pilot. Brought Olive to the billet.

25th November 1943

Went with the boys to Alton, to the movies. Afterwards, I met June and Pat.

26th November 1943

At 2.00 o'clock I went on leave. With my pilot and two other officers, I took a taxi. When I arrived in London, I went to the factory first. The to my house. In the evening, dancing in Manor Place. It was a band of 14 people. N.F.S. Broadcasting Band.

27th November 1943

Today six years ago, was my Bar Mitzvah. In the morning, I went to Mrs. Garf, a good friend of mine, who came a short time ago from Germany to England.

28th November 1943

At 6.40 in the morning, I arrived in Newcastle. At 7.30 I went by train to Morpeth, where I will stay with the Norman family during my leave. Maureen was waiting for me at the station. First, I had breakfast. Then I went to sleep until dinner. In the evening I went to the movies with Maureen and her brother Allon.

29th November 1943

In the evening I've been to the movies with Maureen and Allon. 'Casablanca' with Humphrey Bogart and Ingrid Bergman. A fantastic film.

30th November 1943

In the afternoon I am going by bus to Newcastle with Maureen. We went dancing there in the 'Oxford'. I've met an old girlfriend. Iris Minnon (23). Made an appointment with her for coming Thursday. After the dance at the cinema. 'Dixie' with Bing Crosby. Nice film. Then we went to Morpeth again and played cards at home until 12.00 o'clock.

1st December 1943

In the evening I went with Maureen to the movies. 'The Desperados'. After the film, we went to Maureen's house. Met her brother Allon and together we went for a drink. In the Newcastle Inn, we met Mary Simpson (20) and her sister, who is in the W.A.A.F. I've brought them both back home.

2nd December 1943

In the afternoon I went with Allon to Newcastle. Made an excuse at home. Allon told me he is unemployed. I told him I had to meet someone. We went together. At 2.30 we met Iris and her friend Peggy. Peggy had to do some shopping in the afternoon. So the three of us went for dancing. Afterwards, we had a cup of tea in the 'Metropole'. Then we met Peggy again. The four of us went to the cinema. 'Pilot no. 5', with Franchot Tone. After that, we have drunk a glass of beer. Then we bought chips. First, we've brought Allon to the bus. Then we brought Peggy to the train and then I've been going with Iris to her house. I had to come inside... I met her mother, Bird, a Norwegian, Stanley, a Polish man, and another three English soldiers, who all lived in that house. It looks like it was an international house. I stayed with them until...

3rd December 1943

....1.30. Then I left, and I've been sleeping in the Y.M.C.A. where I ordered already a bed yesterday afternoon. At 8.00 o'clock in the morning, I've got breakfast. I had pictures taken. This afternoon I visited the Patterson family. Then by bus back to Morpeth. In the shoemaker's shop was a little woman, Mrs. Agnes (21) Panter. She asked me if I would go with her in the evening to dance, but I had to refuse because this night I was going back to London. At 6.30, I left the Norman family after I offered them my excuse that I should depart for London at 9.00 o'clock. Instead, I went to Newcastle to see Iris and her mother. First, I've sent a telegram to Marie Westhead, my W.R.E.N., that I should meet her tomorrow.

Went to the dance in the 'Oxford' with Iris, her mother, Kathleen, a good friend, and Peggy and her friend. Stayed there until 12.00 o'clock. Then I took Peggy, her mother, and her sister-in-law to the station because they had to go by train. Said goodbye to Iris in the dancing hall. She is a wonderful woman. I took the train at...

4th December 1943

....12.40 in the night and arrived in London at 8.40 o'clock. Went to my house to pick up some money from the bank to pay for my suit. Then I went to the city and had a meal in a kosher restaurant. Afterwards, I met Marie Westhead. We went to the movies and then she came with me to my house. We stayed at home until 8.30 and then I brought her to the station.

5th December 1943 Sunday

This morning I've seen Olive, and we have drunk a cup of coffee at the Naafi. She was happy to see me. In the evening there was a big party, St. Nicolaas party. It's freezing cold today. Much colder than in the North, from where I just came. The party wasn't special, too much to drink. I didn't feel fine. Brought Olive to the billet.

6th December 1943

Today I had a day off. In the afternoon I went to London and went out with Marie (20) and her friend. Went back at 10.00 o'clock.

7th December 1943

I woke up at 4.00 o'clock. Left the house at 4.45. I took the train at 5.30 and arrived at the camp at 8.15. I've gotten worse. In the afternoon, I went to bed. From Marie, I've received a packet with soap.

8th December 1943

In the morning, I've been to the doctor. I'm staying now for a few days under his orders. In the evening there was a dance but because I have a heavy cold I didn't dance.

9th December 1943

In the evening, the Naafi. I still don't feel good. Brought Olive to the billet.

10th December 1943

Went to London. Had to pick up money, broke. I came home in the afternoon. I've done some shopping with Mrs. Bransom. At 6.15 I met Marie. First, we had a meal. Then we went to the movies. At 10.00 I said goodbye to her, and by train, at 10.35 I travelled back to Alton.

11th December 1943

Went to Alton to dance. I didn't have a nice evening.

12th December 1943 Sunday

I've been to the Naafi. Brought Olive to the billet.

14th December 1943

Big party from the people of the kitchen in the camp. It was very good. Much better than the Dutch party last week.

15th December 1943

I've received three letters from Fre. The third letter came from Vittel, France. She is now transferred to Vittel. In the evening I went out with Olive. We went to the movies in Alton. I had seen that film already twice.

16th December 1943

Today I am 19 years. And today, I have been in the army for one year. It doesn't feel like it's my birthday. I've got £ 1.-.-. from Bill Boutelje to use for my new uniform. 5/[25p]- from Mr. and Mrs. Bransom. In a year, I've written 450 letters and received 387 letters.

18th December 1943

In the evening, I danced with Olive.

20th December 1943

In the evening I am in Alton with my friend Jimmy de Peter. We went to the movies. 'Hit the Ice', with Bud Abbott and Lou Costello. Fantastic film. I've laughed the whole time. At 9.30 we went back to the camp.

21st December 1943

I've been to the cinema in the camp.

22nd December 1943

I broke up with Olive. She became too serious. She wanted to break up with a boyfriend who she had known already for five years. I didn't like that. However, we will stay good friends, and I will take her out as usual. If she will not break up with that boy, I will go out again with her as I did.

23rd December 1943

Went to London to pick up my new uniform. In the evening to the Co-op. Afterwards, I went with an old friend, George Bats, who is now in the R.A.F., to another dance.

Audrey (18). A wonderful girl stood with her under the mistletoe.

24th December 1943

Today it's Mr. Bransom's birthday. 'Cafe Continental' in the Naafi. Very nice. I've received today a Christmas present from Marie Westhead (20). One hundred cigarettes.

25th December 1943

It's Christmas. I've got a day off at 12.00 o'clock. I've been to London. Had dinner at home. In the afternoon, the Benavente family came to visit me. I went away at 8.15. Arrived in Alton at 11.00 o'clock and drove back to the camp by bike. There was a Christmas party still going on. I didn't dance and didn't drink.

26th December 1943 Sunday

In the evening, Naafi. After 9.30, I stayed and talked with Mary, Mabel, and Joyce until 11.15.

27th December 1943

Today it's Boxing Day. Another day off. I've been to London again. In the evening, I went dancing in the Co-op. Joan, my ex-girlfriend, was there because she is on sick leave. She is engaged with a boy who is in Persia now. I've drunk a beer with her, and after the dance, I walked with her for a while.

29th December 1943

Again I've got a day off and again I've been to London. That's three days in a row and cost me a lot of train tickets. First what I did was dancing in the afternoon at the Covent Garden. Met Jean there. I made an appointment with her for my next leave. Afterwards, I go to Chelsea. By a misunderstanding, I've missed Marie. Then I took the bus and went to Hackney to visit that Jewish girl Joyce Kersh, who I met last month. Had a very nice evening there with her father, mother, and sister. At 11.30, Joyce and her father brought me to the train that goes to Liverpool Street.

30th December 1943

I arrived in Liverpool Street at 12.20. From there, I took a taxi to Waterloo Station. I slept in The Union Jack Club. At 6.00 this morning, I've taken the train back to Alton. Worked the whole day in the Officers Mess.

1st January 1944

Today it's New Year, and I hope that the war we go on quicker so that we will get the chance to see the end of the war in the future.

Another party in the camp. Today I also received a Christmas present from Marie (20). A bottle of hair gel 'Evening in Paris'. Good stuff.

3rd January 1944

I've been to Alton with Joop Velleman and Teddie Aartsen. We went to the movies. Nice film, 'Five Graves to Cairo'.

4th January 1944

This evening I've been to the movies in the camp with Olive. The day after tomorrow, Thursday, I go on leave. Today I received a letter from Marie. She is in the hospital. She has an eye infection.

5th January 1944

Went dancing in the camp. I've met Minnie (21). I danced with her the whole evening. After the dance, I will bring her to the billet if it's possible for her, then we will go to Alton tomorrow.

6th January 1944

I'm not on leave. Went to Alton with Joop Velleman. Minnie couldn't come. Went to the movies, but I walked out. A terrible bad film.

7th January 1944

Went on leave. I arrived in London at 6.30 p.m. I went with the bus to Hackney. I visited Joyce and her family. Had a fantastic meal. Chicken soup, chicken with chips and after that a lovely pastry. And then cake and tea. I had a great evening. I came back home at...

8th January 1944

...1.30 o'clock this morning. I went to bed and woke up at 9.00 o'clock. I've listened to the gramophone. Then to Waterloo Station to pick up the suitcase that I left there yesterday evening. In the afternoon, I met Jean (20). To the movies, after that, I had a meal, and then I went to the Battersea Town Hall to dance... came back home at...

9th January 1944 Sunday

...12.55 this morning. Went to bed until 9.00 o'clock. Woke up, washed, shaved, ate something, dressed up, and went to Joyce's house. I arrived there at 12.00 o'clock. We went out. Had a meal at Kahn. Then to Finsbury Park, to the movies. When we came out of the cinema, we met Bill and Kurt. Had a meal with the four of us. Kurt didn't feel well, and he went back home. Bill, Joyce, and I went to the city to 'Willesley's' dinner dance. At 10.00 o'clock we went to Joyce's house. We had a cup of tea quickly and went by train back to Liverpool Street. From there I've been walking to the 'Elephant'. From there, with the night tram back home. I arrived at my house at...

10th January 1944

...1.45 this morning. I've been to the firm in the afternoon. After that, I've been to broadcasting with Emile, that Belgian boy who has worked at our firm but now joined the Belgian Navy. Then had a meal at Lyons Corner House. Afterwards, I went to Joyce's house. I've been to the movies with Joyce. Afterwards, to her house to drink a cup of tea. At 11.45 by train to Liverpool Street. I was back home at...

11th January 1944

...1.30. I went with Mrs. Bransom and little Rita to the movies.
13th January 1944

In the afternoon, I've been to Cricklewood. I visited Mrs Garf. Then to Uxbridge. Met Elsie Cragg there. First, we had a meal together, then we went for a walk, then to the dance. A fantastic band. Nice evening. It's far away. I was back at home at...

14th January 1944

...1.20 this morning. This morning I've let taken my picture. This afternoon I stayed at home because tonight I'm going back to the camp. Joy came to us to drink a cup of tea. I've bought a vase for

Joyce's mother. At 8.30, I left home, and Joyce brought me to the train.

15th January 1944

Today the match Holland-Belgium. Result: 3-2. For Holland. A friend of mine from the camp, Tony Effern, has made two goals for Holland. In the evening, I've been to Farnham with two boys. It was nothing.

16th January 1944 Sunday

In the morning at 11.30, we've got 'stand down'. Went to London with Maurice Goudeketting. We arrived in London at 2.30 o'clock. Ordered a bed in the Union Jack Club. Then to Joyce's house. She was going to the movies. Mrs. Kersh had made lovely food. Suddenly there came a terrible fog. Joyce came back home at 5.30. We played cards together until 9.00 o'clock. Mrs Kersh had made supper. We left at 11.00 o'clock. Mr. Kersh and Joyce have brought us to the train. At 11.45, the train arrived; it was still terrible foggy. At...

17th January 1944

....12.15 we arrived at Liverpool Street. From there, we had to walk to Waterloo Station. Slept until 5.00 o'clock. We went back by train at 6.00. Arrived at the camp at 8.30. The sergeant of the Sailors was waiting for me. At 9.00 o'clock, I was already on roll call. Had to come to the Commander. Tomorrow I will get the result. The reason for the roll call was: 1. Wasn't there on Sunday morning, so I couldn't have known that on Monday morning, I had to light the heaters. 2. I was eight and a half hours late from 'stand down'. 3. I didn't report that I had left the camp.

In the evening to the movies in the camp. 'random Harvest'. A fantastic film with Ronald Colman and Greer Carson. I've called Joyce. She is afraid that I will be punished very hard. I think that too.

18th January 1944

This morning I got the result. Five days light arrest. And two hours per day of criminal duty. So I got off cheap. Tomorrow morning I must light the heaters.

21st January 1944

Today mama has become 56 years. I wish her a happy birthday. I received a letter from Fre.

23rd January 1944

Yesterday evening the punishment was over. At 8.00 o'clock in the morning, I started to walk because I'm going to London. I've had a free ride to Alton. At 10.30 I arrived in London. I went to Joyce's house. Went with her father to his sister-in-law. Very nice people. In the afternoon, I went to the movies with Joyce, her mother, and her father. Afterwards, tea and supper. Joyce has brought me to the train. I've eaten so much today that I don't feel good at all. They gave me a big piece of cake and two apples. I had given them oranges, nuts that I got from my aircrew ration, and powder voor Joyce. I've had a wonderful day.

26th January 1944

Went dancing in the Naafi.

27th January 1944

I went to the movies in the camp. 'The Edge of Darkness'. A wonderful film about the resistance in Norway.

28th January 1944

I've been to Alton to the cinema. Bob Hope in 'They Got Me Covered'. Not as nice as usual.

30th January 1944 Sunday

In the evening to the cinema in the camp. 'Girl Trouble', with Joan Bennett and Don Ameche. I've brought Olive to the billet for the first time in 5 days. Had an exam today on guns. I got 95%, and I was one of the best.

31st January 1944

Went to Alton Olive. First, we went to the movies and then we had a glass of beer. Strange for me because I drink almost never these days. The film was very nice. 'White Captive'. A coloured film. I brought Olive to the billet. Today I received a nice package from Joyce. Sixty cigarettes, one pound of apples, two cakes, sweets, chocolate, and stamps. Beautiful present.

1st February 1944

In the evening to the movies with Olive. 'China', with Loretta Young and Alan Ladd. A nice film.

2nd February 1944

I had a day off. I've picked up Joyce from work. Then I had a meal at her home. I've got a beautiful pipe from her with 2 ounces of tobacco. I got from her father a lighter. Father dinner Joyce has brought me to the train.

4th February 1944

Bad weather this morning. I've got another day off. Went back home. Had a meal at home, then I bought a pair of socks at the Headquarters. I went to Paula (21), a W.A.A.F. girlfriend of mine who is on leave now. I had tea and cake at her house. Then we went to the movies. 'They Flew Alone', with Ann Naegle, Robert Newton. Afterwards, she brought me to the train. ????

5th February 1944

Today I made my first trip with Mr. Neussink. It was not too bad. In the evening to the movies. 'The Gentle Sex'. A film about the A.T.S. It was rather funny. Today I received a message from Fre. It looks like everything is okay.

6th February 1944

Today I've made a second trip. In the afternoon I got two days off. Went back home. Arrived there at 8.00 o'clock. Joyce was there. I brought her home, and I slept there.

9th February 1944

This afternoon I made a third trip. In the evening, I dance in the Naafi. Brought Olive to the billet.

10th February 1944

I've been flying to the new camp. In the evening I went there to a classical concert with Maurice. We walked out there. Met Penny, the sister of Joan (1942).

R.A.F. Station, Dunsfold, Surrey
The 11th of February, 1944

Today Mrs. Bransom has become 35 years. I've been to a little place not far from here with Maurice and two other boys. Cranley, first to the movies and afterward we have drunk a couple of beers.

The 12th of February, 1944

In the evening, I went out. I went dancing in the same village. Nice evening.

The 13th of February, 1944, Sunday

In the afternoon, I've got 'stand down'. I went with Maurice to Guildford. First to the movies. Then we had a meal... after that, we went into all the cafes, and I became terrible drunk.

The 14th of February, 1944

Today I've made my 4th trip. This afternoon at 4.00 o'clock I went on leave. I will spend my leave at Joyce's house.

The 15th of February, 1944

Woke up in the afternoon at 2.00 o'clock. Joyce came back home early. First, we went to the firm, after that to the movies. 'This is the Army'. Very nice film. Then we had a meal at Lyons. We met there an American of Hungarian origin. A Jewish boy.

The 16th of February, 1944

I've been sleeping this afternoon until 5.00 o'clock. At 6.30 I went to the movies with Joyce and Bill Boutelje. 'Top Man', with Donald O'Connor and Richard Dix, and 'Behind the Rising Sun', with Marco. Both are good films.

The 17th of February, 1944

In the afternoon I've been dancing in Covent Garden. I danced the whole afternoon with one girl, Stella 2as her name. In the evening I went dancing in The Royal Tottenham. I took a taxi to go home.

The 18th of February, 1944

Today I visited the Bransom family. In the afternoon, I went with Mrs. Bransom to the movies. 'Thank Your Lucky Star'. Dina Shore, the best singer in America, played in this film. In the evening I went to a dance that was organised by Mr. Bransom. In between, I've been drinking a glass of beer with Pam, an old girlfriend of mine. After that, Joan Hearn (1942) came, and I danced with her until the end. I had to walk a long time, after that with the underground. Then I walked again to Dalston. Then there was an air raid alarm. It was heavy—the heaviest one since 1941. From Dalston, I took a taxi which brought me to Joyce's house.

The 19th of February, 1944

In the afternoon I've been to the football with Joyce. Arsenal 7 - Luton 1. England beats Scotland with 6-2. In the evening I've been dancing in the 'Royal' with Joyce. Came home in a taxi.

The 21st of February, 1944

This evening my leave is over. I went this afternoon to the movies with Joyce. Went back to Dunsfold at 8.45.

The 22nd of February, 1944

I played the evening ping pong with Maurice in the Naafi. Afterwards, we went to the cinema in the camp.

23rd of February 1944

Tomorrow I will be transferred because I don't fly operational now. This is because my telegraphist, Neussink, will leave the hospital tomorrow. It's a pity that I must leave Maurice, but there is nothing to do about it. In the evening we went dancing in Guildford. Ann (21) and Lily (23) brought us to the bus.

24th of February 1944

At 8.30 p.m. I arrived at the camp after travelling the whole day.

R.A.F. Stanton Morley, Norfolk

25th of February 1944

In the evening, I stayed in the Naafi. The dance band played a classic concert just like they are playing at Lyons in London, with light music. It was very nice. After the concert, I met a W.A.A.F. Val Adams (19). I've brought her to the billet.

It's a nice camp. It was already built before the war. Everything here is close together, so you don't have to walk far. We don't have to do something only to maintain the building. The whole day there is hot water so you can wash your clothes or take a bath whenever you want.

26th of February 1944

I've got a day off. I went to Norwich. In the afternoon I went dancing in the 'Sampson'. With Eileen. In the evening, I went to the movies with Doris Spurrell, my other ex-girlfriend. Then I had a meal with Doris at her house, and then I went back to the Y.M.C.A and have slept there.

27th of February 1944

Woke up at 11.00 o'clock. I've been playing billiards with a soldier until 2.00 o'clock. I had a meal, and then I went to Doris. At 6.00 o'clock we went to the cinema. Afterwards again we had a meal at her house. The back to the Y.MCA. and I've slept there again.

28th of February 1944

At 7.00 I went back to the camp with a bus of the workers. In the evening, there was a dance in the camp, and I've been the whole evening with Val. It was very nice.

29th of February 1944

I've been with Val to Dereham, the most nearby village. First, we went to the movies. 'Escape to Danger'. Then we've eaten an egg in the restaurant that's especially for the forces. At 10.00 o'clock we went back to the camp by bus. Had a nice evening.

1st of March 1944

Yesterday evening I've been to the movies in the camp with Val. 'Bataan' with Robert Taylor. Walked out after the first half. Then we had a meal in the Naafi.

3rd of March 1944

I went to the Y.M.C.A. with Val, about a 10-minute walk from the camp. The whole evening we had a nice conversation.

4th of March 1944

I went to Dereham. First, I had a meal. After that, I danced. Brought Lyn (24) back home.

5th of March 1944 Sunday

Went to the movies in the camp with Val. 'Life of Emile Zola'. I saw this film almost 7 years ago in Belgium. There was a play in the camp, but we walked out, we didn't like it.

6th of March 1944

I've received a letter from mama, and she asks me if I should get an English passport for her. I went to the movies with Val. 'Bluebird's Eight Wife' with Gary Cooper and Claudette Colbert.

7th of March 1944

Today I've had an 'escape' exercise. That is: a bus is driving you somewhere, you don't know where, the curtains in the bus are closed, about 7 till 8 miles away from the camp. You have to go out of the bus together with another boy, and then you must try to go back to the camp without being caught by the police, the Home Guard, or the R.A.F. Regiment, who all were looking for us because they were informed. I did come back, but I walked for 4 hours. I was in a cafe for one and a half hours with a couple of other boys who I saw there. So half-drunk, we had to come back. Nearby the camp, I went on alone. The others walked on the main road. I walked through a field and had to go into the river that surrounds the camp. So I arrived at the camp without being caught but was soaking wet. In the evening, I stayed in the Naafi with Val. Tomorrow we will go together to Norwich. Both of us have a day off.

8th of March 1944

I went to Norwich with Val. But it wasn't very nice. First, we had a meal, then we went shopping, and we have bee to the movies twice.

9th of March 1944

I played football from 4.30-6.30. I played as a goalkeeper and hurt my arm. After the match, I went to the cinema in the camp.

10th of March 1944

There was a dance event in the camp. Although I was very tired, I had a nice evening with Val. I danced a lovely tango with Penny.

11th of March 1944

Went to Dereham. Val and I went with the R.A.F. band who was going to play there. There was a fight, one of our boys with an Englishman. Have eaten a lovely egg in the canteen. After the dance, we went back to the camp together with the band. I've brought Val as usual to the billet.

12th of March 1944

In the evening, I had to spend a few hours with Val because she was on duty.

15th of March 1944

In the evening I went to the movies in the camp with Val.

17th of March 1944

In the evening I went to a nice coloured film with Val. 'Arabian Nights'.

18th of March 1944

I've been with Val to Dereham. It wasn't nice. It was a pity.

19th of March 1944 Sunday

Went to the cinema this evening with Val.

20th of March 1944

Today my old telegraphist Jan de Jong and my friend Kuipers didn't come back. In the evening there was a dance in the camp, but I didn't like it, because all the time I had been thinking of the boys.

21st of March 1944

Today it's the birthday of the father of Joyce. In the evening, there was a big dance event in the Naafi. I won the first prize in singing. The song was 'Chattanooga 'Choo Choo'.

22nd of March 1944

I played football for the team of our station against the aircrew. We lost 2-1. I've made the only goal for the station team. It was the first goal that I've made this season. In the evening I went with Val to the movies and then to the ENSA show in the Naafi. Very nice.

23rd of March 1944

I've got a message from Fre. I played netball with the W.A.A.F.s at 5.00 o'clock. It's a kind of korfball. We won 17-9. I've made 14 goals. I went to bed at 8.00 o'clock.

24th of March 1944

In the evening I went to Norwich. I've met Vera (22). I've been dancing in the 'Lido'. A very nice dance hall.

25th of March 1944

I've been to Dereham with Val... first, we were going to the movies. Then we've eaten a lovely egg. At 9.30 we went back to the camp by bus.

26th of March 1944, Sunday

Today it's Bill's birthday. It's beautiful weather. In the afternoon I will go cycling for an hour.

27th of March 1944

At 5.00 o'clock I went to the movies with Lilian (24) because Val had the night shift. Then to the Naafi and went dancing with Lilian. Val came a little bit later. Of course, I was in a 'mess'. Val left at

11.00 o'clock, and after the dance, I brought Lilian to the billet. I will never do such a thing again.

28th of March 1944

At 2.00 o'clock I left the camp for two days. Arrived in London at 7.00 o'clock. Went to the house of Joyce.

30th of March 1944

Joyce made a phone call with Mrs. Bransom in the morning. Mrs. Bransom has told her that she is expecting a baby again, who will be born around November. I will become an uncle for the second time. Joyce and her mother brought me to the train late in the afternoon because the two days had passed by already. I arrived in Norwich at 6.20, and then I went dancing in the Y.M.C.A. with Eileen. Then I brought her back home. I stayed in the Y.M.C.A. overnight.

31st of March 1944

At 7.20, I left Norwich. Arrived at the camp at 9.00 o'clock. Exactly on time. I spent the evening with Val in the Naafi. We were glad to be with each other again.

1st of April 1944

In the evening I was in the cinema with Val. We've seen a nice film.

2nd of April 1944, Sunday

I've been to the movies. Val is on the night shift. I went to the room at 9.00 o'clock and played cards for a few hours.

3rd of April 1944

In the evening I've been dancing in the Naafi with Val.

4th of April 1944

To the movies in the camp with Val.

The 6th of April, 1944

I've played football for the English aircrew. Aircrew 2 - R.A.F. Regiment 6. It wasn't a nice match. In the evening to the cinema with Val.

8th of April 1944

I received an invitation to a big dance event in the evening from the people of the 'cookhouse'. It was very nice, and I had a nice evening.

9th of April 1944, Sunday

In the evening to the cinema with Val.

10th of April 1944

In the evening to the cinema with Val. I've almost nothing else to do than go to the cinema. Today it was a year ago that I became an air gunner.

The 11th of April, 1944

This afternoon I've left the camp together with 2 of our boys because again I am going on leave. The three of us went first to the movies in Norwich. Then we had a meal in the 'Curat House'. Then we went dancing in the 'Lido'. I met May (25). Made an appointment with her for Thursday next week after I come back from leave.

13th of April 1944

In the evening, I've been out with Marie Westhead, so I had to send a telegram to Elsie that I couldn't come.

14th of April 1944

In the afternoon I went dancing in the Covent Garden. In the evening to the cinema with Joyce. 'The Sullivan's. A very nice film. I went to bed at 1.00 because Joyce wanted to talk with me about something important.

15th of April 1944

In the afternoon I've been looking to the Cup Final of football. Charlton 3 - Chelsea 1. It was a good match although the weather was bad. Then I met Joyce in the city, and with the four of us, we went to the movies. 'Tender Comrade', with Ginger Rogers. Then we had a nice meal, and we went home by taxi. Stayed at Joyce's house overnight.

16th of April 1944, Sunday

I went to the market with my father of Joyce and bought a new suitcase for £ 1.6.6 [£1.33p]. In the afternoon I went to the city with Joyce. Today I received a letter from Val.

17th of April 1944

In the afternoon I've been to the movies with Mr. and Mrs. Bransom. '£ 100 Window' and 'In Old Oklahoma' with John Wayne, Martha Scott, and Albert Dekker. I spent the evening at Joyce's house. (Joyce, me, - - -M.G.)

18th of April 1944

In the afternoon, Mrs. Bransom, Joyce, and her mother have brought me to the train. I was back in the camp at 8.00 o'clock. I picked up Val and walked to the village with her and with my friend Jimmy de Preter and his girlfriend Madge, and we drank some beer.

20th of April 1944

Went with Val to Dereham. We had a few drinks and went to the movies.

21st of April 1944

I've been to the movies in the camp with Val.

23th of April 1944

Went with Val to the little river that surrounds the camp, and Val has been swimming for a little while. It's beautiful weather but too cold.

24th of April 1944

Today my punishment started that I've got because I didn't do the 'escape' exercise the day before yesterday. Jimmy didn't either, so the both of us got 5 days of light arrest. So I've to report myself every hour in the guardroom between 5.00 o'clock and 10.00 o'clock. Anyway, I went to the dance and reported myself every hour. I'm in a bad mood.

25th of April

I've been to the movies in the camp and reported myself again every hour.

26th of April 1944

I've received a letter from Joyce today. It is over between us. It's her mother's birthday today. This evening Val is on the night shift.

28th of April 1944

This evening my punishment has come to an end. I received a strange letter from Maurice about him and Joyce. Went to the cinema with Val.

29th of April 1944

I've been to Dereham with Val. Then we had a meal, and we went back by bus at 10.00 o'clock.

30th of April 1944, Sunday

For the first time since the 14th of February, I've flown today. I've got a kind of ringing in my right ear. In the evening to the cinema. Then we went for a walk with the 6 of us. Y.M.C.A. and pub.

1st of May 1944

This morning I've been to the doctor because of my ear. I'm not allowed to fly until my ear is better. I must steam 3 times a day. In the evening dance in the Naafi.

2nd and 3rd of May 1944

I've stayed in the billet. Nothing to report.

4th of May 1944

Nothing to report. I've been playing cards in the billet.

5th of May 1944

At 2.00 o'clock I went to London. I came back home at 7.30.

6th of May 1944

In the morning, I visited Miss Pappenheim. In the afternoon I went to the football. Millwall 4 - Chelsea 2. A nice match. In the evening, the Co-op. Met some old friends. I've brought Maureen a little while to her house and made an appointment with her for tomorrow afternoon.

7th of May 1944

In the morning, I've taken Rita to the Benavente family, her grandparents. In the afternoon I've been to the city with Maureen. To the movies. 'Melody Inn'. Then I went with her to her house, and we drank tea. In the evening we went walking.

8th of May 1944

At 8.10 I left London. I was back in the camp at 1.45. In the evening I've been dancing with Val in the Naafi.

The 9th of May, 1944

In the evening I've been to the movies in the camp with Val and Maurice, who have been placed here for 14 days. 'The Corsican Brothers' and 'Taxi Mister'. Nice films.

10th of May 1944

Today it's 4 years ago that the war has started.

11th of May 1944

In the afternoon, I've been to Norwich on the back of the motorcycle. The first time that I'm sitting on a motorcycle since my trip from Antwerp to Amsterdam 8 years ago.

13th of May 1944

At 12.00 o'clock I went on leave. I arrived in London at 7.00 o'clock. Went to the Co-op. Today it was 4 years ago that I left Belgium.

The 14th of May, 1944

This afternoon I went to Joyce and visited the family. Then I went all by myself, although Joyce wanted to come with me. Went to the cinema. 'Higher and Higher', with Frank Sinatra, my favourite singer. Then I've been to Lyons and then back home. I came home at 9.15. Instead of going to Nottingham on Wednesday, I'm already going on Tuesday.

15th of May 1944

I've done today some different business. In the evening, I've been to the movies with Maureen Nunn (18). 'Four Jills in a Jeep'. A nice film.

16th of May 1944

I arrived in Nottingham at 2.00 o'clock. I've been dancing right away. It wasn't nice. I even don't know where I must go in the evening. Again I've been dancing. I met Margaret and Jackie (A.T.S.). At 11.00 o'clock I was in bed already.

17th of May 1944

I've been going to the family of Elsie Cragg. Got there a cup of tea. In the evening I went to the city with the married daughter Joyce, because she had to see her friends. I've seen the film 'Madame Curie', Greer Garson and Walter Pidgeon. Went to a little dance but I only had a meal there.

The 18th of May, 1944

In the afternoon I went dancing. I've met Mrs. Dorothy Allen (23). We've been eating together. Then we went to a nice show. 'Hit the Deck'. A show about the Navy. Then I bought a sandwich and a glass of beer and brought Dorothy to the train.

The 19th of May, 1944

In the afternoon, I went to the Cragg family. I've been to the city with Mrs. Cragg and the youngest daughter Barbara (15) to do some shopping for the wedding of their oldest daughter Phyllis.

The 20th of May 1944

Olive has come for a 'day off'. I took her and her brother to the wedding of Phyllis Cragg. To the church, then the reception and afterwards with Olive to her house and met her parents. At 8.00 o'clock, I brought Olive away and met Dorothy. Brought her to the train at 10.00 o'clock. She lives in Loughborough, 15 miles from here.

The 21st of May 1944, Sunday

At 7.45 I'm going to London. At 5.00 o'clock we left London, back to the camp. Maureen has brought me to the train. I stayed in Norwich overnight.

22nd of May 1944

I came back this morning at 9.00 o'clock. Tomorrow I will be transferred to Finmere. I've given Val 2 boxes of powder, 5/6, 70 cigarettes, and a coupon for a pair of stockings. In the evening I dance. I stayed with Val until...

The 23rd of May, 1944

....1.30. Today, four years ago, I arrived in England. We left for Finmere.

24th of May 1944

Today the lessons have started. We will stay here for 6 weeks. Jimmy de Preter is in my crew. I'll have to study very hard because then I can make a promotion faster. This evening I will go dancing. Went to the dancing in the nearest village. At 12.00 o'clock I went back to the camp with 2 Canadian Officers.

25th of May 1944

I had lessons during the whole day. This evening I will write letters.

The 26th of May 1944

In the evening, after the lessons, I went to the cinema. 'Cargo of Innocents', with Brian Donlevy and Robert Taylor. At the last moment, I changed my mind and went to Buckingham together with Pieter and Murray, who I met yesterday evening. First, we had a drink. Then we went dancing. I met Margery (21) from the N.F.S. After that, I met Eileen (20). I've been flirting with her for 15 minutes. At the end of the dance, I made an appointment with a Naafi girl who worked here once a week. Mary.

27th of May 1944

In the evening, I went to Buckingham with two French boys, Robert and André. Margery (21) was also there, she stayed the whole evening with me, and I brought her back home after the dance.

28th of May 1944 Sunday

Today it's very hot. Tonight I will stay writing letters and washing my clothes.

29th of May 1944

This afternoon I received a message from Fre that she and mama were ready to come to England, but at the last minute, it was postponed. In the evening I went to the village. I made an appointment with a W.A.A.F. for tomorrow evening. The whole evening I danced with one girl, her name is Mandy (19). I've brought her to the billet after the dance.

30th of May 1944

I've picked up my bike from the station. I had a flat tire, and I fixed it at the station.

31st of May 1944

This afternoon I've left the lessons and have been a little shopping in Buckingham. Mary, the W.A.A.F girl, didn't come. So I went back to the camp. I was in bed at 10.00 o'clock.

1st of June 1944

In the evening, I go for a ride with Winnie (22). A very strange girl.

2nd of June 1944

This afternoon I have done an escape exercise with my pilot. I walked for one and a half hours but arrived back in the camp without being caught. In the evening, I dance in the camp.

3rd of June 1944

I've been dancing in Buckingham. I've brought Olive (21) back to her house. I've made an appointment for coming Tuesday. It was a nice evening.

4th of June 1944

I've been staying in the camp. Terrible weather. I've been playing cards in the Sergeants Mess.

5th of June 1944

This evening I went to the cinema in the army camp. I've seen the film before, but it was worth the effort to see the film again. 'Stormed Weather'. I've seen again the Naafi girl, and we made an appointment for coming Wednesday. Today I got a message from mama.

6th of June 1944

I've been going to Buckingham. Have been to the cinema with Olive (21). Afterwards, we ate chips and drank a cup of tea. Bad weather.

7th of June 1944

I've been to Tingewick with Mary (21). Have spent an hour in the pub.

8th of June 1944

Went to the movies in the camp this evening. 'One Dangerous Night', with Warren Williams and Eric Blore.

9th of June 1944

This evening I've been dancing in Buckingham. I had to see Mary. I danced with her the whole evening. Made an appointment for tomorrow evening.

10th of June 1944

Went dancing with Mary in Bucks. Had a nice evening. We couldn't get our bicycle chains open and were busy with that for a while.

11th of June 1944

I've been to an ENSA show in the camp. It wasn't very special, but the evening passed by in this way.

12th of June 1944

Today I received a message from mama. This evening there will be a big dance event in the Sergeants Mess. I must pick up Mary from her camp at 10.00 o'clock because she's working until that time. Went to the dance. I've been drinking with a few people. At 10.00 I pick up Mary. A little bit later, when Jimmy, my friend and air gunner, was talking with Mary, I took Mandi (21) outside and flirted a little bit. At...

14th of June 1944

....1.00 o'clock. Was back in the camp and in bed at 2.00 o'clock. This evening at 7.30 I met Mary, and we went to an ENSA show in her camp. It was a fantastic show. After the show, I've been talking with Mary. /-. - -/ times. Stayed with her until...

15th of June 1944

....1.50 this morning. Then I walked back to the camp because I had a flat tire. I will stay tonight writing letters. Mary is transferred to Bletchley.

16th of June 1944

Already this evening I've received the first letter from Mary. She is about 12 miles from here, and I will visit her once. This evening I've been to the dance in Tingewick. It was a little bit better. (Change 47 yrs. Son 25). Came back to the camp together with Jimmy.

18th of June 1944, Sunday

This evening I stayed home to study for the exam.

The 19th of June, 1944

It was today, 9 years ago, that my late father passed away. Of course, I stayed in the camp. This night I've flown for the first time in the night. Received a letter from Fre.

20th of June 1944

Today I've got the results of the exam. I became no. Seven from the 36 and got 84%. The first one had 89%. So I did it perfectly. Today a few boys from Stanton Morley arrived here, and they told me that Val is going on leave. She should come here to Finmere coming Monday. I will be very happy. This evening I had to stay here because of the night flights.

21st of June 1944

Night flights.

22nd of June 1944

I've been to London. I was at home for a few hours. Val is going on leave today, and I've picked her up unexpectedly. I talked with her for just 15 minutes. Monday and Tuesday, she will come to the camp. When I came back to the camp, I arranged a room for her. When I came back, I heard that we must make night flights. I got a severe reprimand from the pilot.

23rd of June 1944

I've been this evening to the dance in Tingewick. I had to go at 11.30 because I had a night flight again. I've brought Hilda (21) W.A.A.F. to the billet

24th and 25th of June, Sunday

Nothing to report.

26th of June 1944

This afternoon Val has come to Finmere.

27th of June 1944

This morning I went to London with Val. Everything went wrong today. I arrived at 1.30 in London. Had to go back at 6.11 o'clock. I didn't go back because there was an air raid alarm. I went back by train at 8.30 o'clock. Arrived at the camp at 10.30 o'clock. There was a night flight. I was one hour late. I went to the pilot, who was ready for take-off. The only thing that he said was: 'Push back'. And tomorrow, I must report to the Squadron Leader.

28th of June 1944

I've been to the Squadron Leader. He was very angry. In the evening there was a dance in the Concert Hall. I won 40 cigarettes. I've brought Mandi (21) to the billet.

29th of 1944

This afternoon Val has come again. In the evening I've been to the pub with her for an hour. I've been staying with Val until...

30th of June 1944

....1.30 in the morning. The whole day I had to do air firing. I finished at 6.00 o'clock. I am coming to Val at 8.00 o'clock. Went to the dance in Tingewick. After the dance, I stayed with Val until 3.45 in the morning. (- . - -   - - -) times.

1st of July 1944

Val went back to London at 8.00 o'clock and used my bike to go to the station. This afternoon I've got off for 48 hours. I went to Loughborough. Arrived there at 7.00 o'clock. I went to Dorothy, but she wasn't at home. Rented a room in the 'Kings Head Hotel', the nicest hotel in town. First, I washed and shaved, and then I went to the dance in the Town Hall. Joan Stevenson (25), a friend of Dorothy, was there. I danced with her for the whole evening and brought her back home.

2nd of July 1944 Sunday

I've been to Dorothy's house. I met her parents there. Stayed there for dinner. With the four of us, we played cards in the afternoon. Then we had a cup of tea, and in the evening, we went to a pub somewhere. Had a nice day.

3rd of July 1944

I've been to the movies in the afternoon. 'Girl Crazy', with Mickey Rooney and Judy Garland. In the evening, I travelled back to Finmere. Received a message from Fre.

The 4th of July 194

Suddenly I had to leave Finmere in the afternoon because I had to go to the Squadron. First, I've got a day off and so I went to the Bransom family.

5th of July 1944

In the afternoon I had a meal in the city. I've been to the headquarters to pick up some money and then to the movies. A very nice film. 'Two Girls and a Sailor', with Harry James and his Orchestra. In the evening I am going to Joyce. I stayed there until 9.30. Then I went back home.

6th of July 1944

This morning I brought £ 40 to the bank and so now I have £ 150 altogether. I left London at 1.00 o'clock together with my pilot Mr. Collee. In the afternoon, we arrived at the camp.

7th of July 1944

At 12.30 I've seen Val. Of course, I was very happy and so was she. I've been going to dance in Cranleigh. It was very nice there. I have to make the best of my time because I can't go out so often in the coming time when I will go flying.

8th of July 1944

Tomorrow I have to go to Stanton Morley together with the crew. We must do a course there. So I won't see Val for 14 days. In the evening I waited for Val and stayed with her until 12.00 o'clock.

9th of July 1944 Sunday

This morning I went to Stanton Morley by car. We were driving through London, and we had a meal at the Chinese. I didn't like it. We arrived in Stanton Morley at 8.00 o'clock.

10th of July 1944

Nothing to report. We played cards in the evening.

11th of July 1944

In the evening, there was a dance in the dancing hall upstairs in the Cookhouse. I've brought Joyce from the Naafi to the billet.

12th of July 1944

I've seen a wonderful ENSA show. Had a very good evening.

13th of July 1944

Nothing to report. In the evening, there was a whist drive in the W.A.A.F.s quarters. Jimmy and I took part in it. In this way, we spend the evening.

14th of July 1944

I had flown this morning. This afternoon I've got off for 48 hours, until Sunday evening. I will go to Norwich. I arrived there at 7.00 o'clock. Went to the 'Lido' to dance there. It was a nice evening. Eileen, my old dance partner, was also there. I had to walk back all the way.

15th of July 1944

I've been sleeping in the Y.M.C.A. until 12.00 o'clock. In the afternoon, I visit my family of Doris. I went back to the city with her mother and sister. I left them in the city. I've seen Barbara (23) and Mrs. Macintosh. I have known her since last year from Attlebridge. I've been to the movies with her. I've taken one pound of cherries. After that, we had a lovely meal, went to a show in the Hippodrome, and brought with me two pounds of strawberries. At 10.00 o'clock Barbara went home by bike. I've had a lovely day.

16th of July 1944

I have been sleeping until 9.30 o'clock. I've had breakfast, and this afternoon I will go to the synagogue. I met Mrs. Wine there. I've been invited to come to her house for a cup of tea. I have been staying there until 8.00 o'clock. Then I went back by bus to Swanton Morley.

17th of July 1944

Dance in the camp.

21st of July 1944

I've seen Val for the first time at 10.30. Last Wednesday, she got engaged to Jock, her real boyfriend. I've given her as a present £ 1 and a box of powder. In the evening I was with her in the Naafi, and afterwards, we went for a walk until 11.00 o'clock. I spent my first night in a tent.

22nd of July 1944

My first operational trip with Mr. Collee. We came back very late.

23rd of July 1944

I was eating with Val in the 'Hatch' before I took pictures for the film news.

24th of July 1944

I've a bad cold. I went flying, although if I went to the doctor, he wouldn't allow me. Today I've made my second trip.

25th of July 1944

I was a petty officer of the watch all day, and I will be that till tomorrow evening. I've got one hour off to go to Val the, opposite the field.

26th of July 1944

Today I've made my 3rd trip. For the first time I've had it flat, Van Leeuwen has been shot.

27th of July 1944

Nothing to report.

28th of July 1944

I've received the message that mama and Fre arrived in Lisbon. I'm very happy.

29th of July 1944

In the evening I've got some free time. I went to Lockwood, a little village nearby. I have been dancing there for an hour.

30th of July 1944

Today I've made my 4th and 5th trip. When I came back from that second one, I went to bed immediately because I was very tired.

31st of July 1944

My best friend Maurice Goudeketting did come back from his rest period. In the evening we went together to Lockwood by motorcycle. We've been drinking Sherry Brandy. It tasted wonderful. We had a nice time.

1st of August 1944

Today I've got a day off. I went with Maurice to London by motorcycle. He has got another month on leave. First, we went to the firm. After that, we went to Covent Garden. After the dance, we've been drinking a beer in the 'Odenino'. Then we went to Folman's to eat something and afterwards to the movies, 'Passage to Marseille'.

http://myfinmere.com/history/history/airfield/airfield.htm

https://sites.google.com/site/derelictionintheshires/military-sites/raf-finmere

https://dunsfoldairfield.org/mitchells-approach-dunsfold-film-discovered/

http://derelictmisc.org.uk/rafbhq.html

https://www.forgottenairfields.com/airfield-attlebridge-1446.html

http://www.ukairfields.org.uk/attlebridge.html

https://www.forces-war-records.co.uk/units/5043/raf-morpeth/

3rd of August 1944

....1.00 o'clock this morning. I made my 6th trip this morning. That makes a total of 10 trips because I've already made 4 trips with Mr. Neussink in February.

4th of August 1944

I've made my 11th and 12th trip today. I've got the message that mama and Fre are already on their way to England.

5th of August 1944

I've made my 13th trip today. After flying, I went to go dancing this evening. I met Lilian there and brought her back again. I was back in the camp at...

The 6th of August, 1944

....2.00 o'clock. This morning I made my 14th trip. And this evening I've made my 15th trip. I've had a heavy trial by fire.

7th of August 1944

I've made my 16th trip today. In the evening, I've been dancing in Lockwood. I've met Lorna Sanders (19) A.T.S. A very nice girl. I've brought her back home and left her at...

8th of August 1944

....1.00 o'clock this morning. At 12.00 I've been to the 'Hatch' for a meal. Immediately after that, I had to go back to the camp, in case of making a flight. This evening I've made my 17th trip. It was a very heavy trip.

9th of August 1944

This morning I made my 18th trip. It has been a terrible trip. Jimmy was badly hurt; May not even make it. There were 7 holes, half a centimetre above my head. The first one has hit my helmet. That has saved me. We had made an emergency landing on the coast, and we got a meal in the Officers Mess there while Jimmy was taken to the hospital. I hope never to experience a trip like this.

10th of August 1944

I've got a day off today. I have been to London to get information about mama and Fre. They arrived yesterday in Liverpool. In the evening, I've been visiting the Kersh family, together with Bill and Kurt. There were 15 people.

11th of August 1944

At 7.15 this morning, Jimmy passed away. Later I went to London because I've got free days until Sunday evening. In the evening I've been dancing in Covent Garden. Afterwards, I go to Lyons to eat something and then go back home.

12th of August 1944

At 13.15, I've taken the train to Devon. I had to stand on the train the whole time. Mother and Fre had just arrived at Cousin Emanuel. It was great to be together again. Mother was very shocked to see me in my uniform. She had a lot to tell me about her experiences, and so did Fre. They both looked good.

13th of August 1944

I woke up at 9.30. I had to go back to the camp at 3.00 o'clock in the afternoon. Again I had to stand the whole time. I arrived at the camp at 12.00 o'clock.

15th of August 1944

Jimmy de Preter will be buried at 11.00 o'clock today. We, the crew, have no permission to go there because there is a chance that we must fly. At least we have sent a wreath, the three of us. This afternoon we flew, but we had to come back. This trip doesn't count.

16th of August 1944

Tomorrow evening I will go on leave. The trip yesterday has been counted for half. That makes a total of 20 because some time ago, I also made a half trip.

17th of August 1944

This afternoon Lorna (A.T.S.) has come to Dunsfold. I couldn't leave before 5.30. Lorna went with me to London, and she has slept in our house with the Bransom family. Late in the evening, we've made a walk because it has been very hot today. - .— —-

18th of August 1944

In the morning I did some shopping with Lorna. In the afternoon I've been to the movies with her. 'Christmas Holiday', with Deanna Durbin and Gene Kelly. Then we had a meal at Lyons Corner House. Then I brought Lorna to the train. Then I went back home. I put on my civilian suit and went dancing in Covent Garden. After the dance, I did eat a little thing.

19th of August 1944

It's my birthday of Fre today. She is now 22. I arrived in the afternoon in Newton Abbot. Mother and Fre were waiting for me at the train station. Went home to drink a cup of tea. At 8.00 o'clock I went dancing for a little hour with Fre.

20th of August 1944

At 6.00 o'clock in the evening, I've been to the movies with Fre. 'Footlight Serenade'. With Victor Mature, John Payne, and Betty Grable. We came back home already at 9.30.

21st of August 1944

I've been to the movies with mama, my niece Yvonne and Fre. 'For Whom the Bell Tolls'. A very nice film with Gary Cooper and Ingrid Bergman. In the evening to dance. I met Linda (24).

22nd of August 1944

In the afternoon I've been to Torquay with mama and Fre. Tomorrow morning I will go to London with Fre.

23rd of August 1944

We arrived in London at 2.30. Immediately we tried to get a job for Fre. We had no success until now. In the evening, we visited Joyce. Fre will stay there for a couple of days. I slept there too last night. Bill and Kurt did come too, and so we had a nice evening all together. Paris has fallen today.

24th of August 1944

Today we tried again to find a job for Fre. One boss did ask her to come back. I bought presents for the Kersh family and a present for Joyce's birthday.

26th of August 1944

Today I've made 2-day trips and a one-night trip. So there are cleft 15. So I couldn't meet Lorna. I will probably see her tomorrow. Val came to see me. She stayed until our start. She wanted to come with us, but that wasn't possible.

27th of August 1944, Sunday

I've seen Lorna at lunchtime. Stayed with her until 1.30. This afternoon I got off until 7.00 o'clock. Sure there will be a night flight. The night flight is cancelled.

28th of August 1944

I've made my 26th trip. Heavy. Still 14.

29th of August 1944

Today it's Joyce's birthday. I visited her in the afternoon and slept in their house.

30th of August 1944

At 1.00 o'clock my friend Maurice came to Joyce also. In the afternoon we went dancing for an hour, and in the evening, we went to the movies with Joyce. I missed my train and had to take one later, the bus had gone already, but I got a free ride to the camp.

31st of August 1944

Today it's Queens Day. This morning I flew to Gloucester to meet the girlfriend of Mr. Boom. While we were landing, the brakes didn't work, so we crashed. Fortunately, none of us were wounded. In the afternoon, we played poker in the Sergeants Mess. We won all the games so. I've won 12.10.-[£12.50p]. and the other Dutch sergeant Van Berkum £ 16.-.-.-. All the other boys have lost. At 5.00 o'clock we left, and I don't think they were willing to see us back. I've been out this evening with Jan Boom and Bum van Berkum. Both were also in the plain this morning. We drank a little bit, and then we went to a little hall where people were dancing, and I've sung there. 'I couldn't sleep a wink last night'.

1st of September 1944

Today I've made my 27th trip. Everything O.K.

2nd of September 1944

In the evening to Lockwood. I've brought Olwyn back home. (28).

3rd of September 1944, Sunday

Today is the beginning of the 6th year of the war. I hope it will be finished next year.

4th of September 1944

Brussels has fallen today. Antwerp 48 km. In the afternoon, I went to Guildford. First, I had a meal. Then I had a meal somewhere else, and then I went dancing for an hour. I've made an appointment with Irene (A.T.S.) for tomorrow evening. Probably I won't go.

5th of September 1944

Went to Guildford with Maurice. I've met a Jewish girl, Kitty.

7th of September 1944

Today I've got off. Went to London with Maurice. We went dancing in Covent Garden and made an appointment there for the evening with the female manager. After the dance, we've been to Lyons Corner House to eat something. We've met there two lovelies W.A.A.F.s. (Irene and Daphny). I was with Daphny (21). Stayed with them until 10.00 o'clock. We brought them to the train, and after that, we walked through the city.

8th of September 1944

Woke up this morning at 4.30. At ss5.30, we took the train, and we were back in the camp at 8.00 o'clock. I've received a letter from mama, she's coming to London today, and she is going to live there in Highbury.

9th of September 1944

I could leave the camp this evening only at 10.00 o'clock. Went to Loxwood, where Lorna was waiting for me. We didn't stay at the dance very long; I brought her home at 11.00 o'clock.

10th of September 1944

Nothing to report today. I've been playing ping pong with Maurice in the Naafi.

11th of September 1944

Today I've made my 29th trip, and probably it will be the last for a long time. I've been hurt when we were flying over Holland. I tried to be strong, but at 7.00 o'clock, three hours after I had been hurt, they helped me to a hospital. Immediately I got emergency surgery.

12th of September 1944

I'm in a Canadian hospital. The first surgery hasn't been successful, and this afternoon I've got a second surgery. I get every three hours injections, and those are terribly painful. I've written to mama and told her in the letter that I felt from my bike, so mama, who is very weak, wouldn't care too much about it.

13th of September

Maurice came to see me; he had brought me oranges.

14th of September 1944

The leader of the camp came to see me. Corporal De Haan, and Sergeant Schwartz from the Canadian Air Force, they came to see me too. Mama and Fre came for an hour in the evening to see me. Tomorrow I'm allowed to lay next to the radio.

15th of September 1944

I don't feel well at all today. Lorna came to visit me in the evening.

16th of September 1944

I didn't sleep all night long. Mama and Fre will come this afternoon. Bill came with them. In Horsham, they've found a place with civilians who let them sleep in their house. That is very nice of them. Tomorrow they can come again to see me.

17th of September 1944

Mama Fre and Bill came again at 2.00 o'clock this afternoon, and so did Joyce and Kurt. Joyce brought me books and Kurt cigarettes. They all left at 7.30.

19th of September 1944

This morning the doctor came to see my leg. He told me it was going well. This afternoon Mary Carroll (21) came to see me together with her Waafi female manager. We were glad to see each other again because I didn't see her since June. I had already rented a room for her to spend two days on Dunsfold, but then I got hurt. It seems there's always something in between when I should see her. She brought me pears, apples, chocolate, and cigarettes. She couldn't stay for a long time because she had to go on a long journey. In the evening, Val (19) came to visit me and brought me chocolate, cigarettes, and peanuts. Also, Maurice came, and he brought me oranges and chocolate. I write down what I receive from people to show how they spoil me. There were 6 girls in 6 weeks, and I hope there will never be two girls at the same time because I don't want to have a fight in the hospital.

20th of September 1944

This morning I've written letters again. I received 28 letters in 4 days. This evening Mr. Colle, Mr. Boom, and Chris de Jong came to visit me. They didn't stay a long time, but I was glad to see them (That's the crew).

21st of September 1944

In the evening, Lorna came again to see me.

22nd of September 1944

This morning I had surgery again, and the doctor stitched up the wound. I had pain the whole day and was glad that there was no one to visit me.

23rd of September 1944

Mama, Fre, and Joyce came to visit me in the afternoon. Also, Mr. Bransom came. He brought me an extra 100 cigarettes from Post no.

26. I belonged to that Post from 1940-1941 during the bombings. I sent them immediately a thank you letter.

I've to stay in bed for another 10 days, and maybe then they will give me permission to come out. Mama and Fre stayed overnight with the same people, and Joyce and Mr. Bransom went back to London.

24th of September 1944

Mama came again this afternoon, and she went back to London at 5.30.

25th of September 1944

At 4.00 o'clock this afternoon, it has been 14 days since I got wounded. I've got today for the last time injections.

26th of September 1944

Today Daphny should have come to see me, but she didn't come. There was a little show this afternoon.

28th of September 1944

We had in our room a cinema showing this afternoon.

29th of September 1944

This evening Lorna came again, and so the evening passed quickly.

30th of September 1944

Mother and Fre did come again. I've got a message that next Monday I will be transferred to an English R.A.F. Hospital.

1st of October 1944 Sunday

This afternoon the doctor removed the stitches from my leg. Mama, Fre, Bill, and Kurt came to visit me. Yesterday evening Mrs. Roberts, the woman where mama sleeps every night, came to see me. There was also a friend with her.

2nd of October 1944

This morning at 11.30, I left the hospital in an ambulance. At 2:30, I arrived at the P.A.H. Hospital, Halton, Buckinghamshire. It's close to the neighbourhood where Mary is living. This evening there was a cinema show in our room. Olwyn (20) came to sit on my bed and keep me company. The title of the film was 'Once upon a time Honeymoon', with Ginger Rogers and Cary Grant. A nice film.

4th of October 1944

This afternoon Daphny came to see me. I was very happy because it's very boring here. She looked very sweet.

5th of October 1944

Today I was allowed for the first time to come out of my bed. I can walk a little bit, but I'm not allowed to walk, because anyhow I have too much weight on my leg. So I'm sitting in my wheelchair.

6th of October 1944

I received a little package from mama this morning. This afternoon I was permitted to sit in my wheelchair for four hours.

7th of October 1944

Mary came this afternoon to see me and brought me all different kinds of things. She brought sugar too, and that's what I'm needed here. She looked sweet. It was really a pity that she had to go.

8th of October 1944, Sunday

Mama and Fre came this afternoon to see me. It won't take long before I'm released from the hospital.

9th of October 1944

This morning the doctor told me that I must go somewhere else. I'm not sure where I'm going.

10th of October 1944

Today it's the birthday of Rita Bransom. She is 3 years now.

11th-14th of October 1944

Nothing to report.

14th of October 1944

I got a pass that allows me to go to Aylesbury. Mary came to the hospital. Together we have been to Aylesbury. We had been drinking a cup of tea and then we had to stay in a queue for 55 minutes to see a movie. But it was a fantastic film. 'Cover Girl'. With Rita Hayworth and Gene Kelly. Afterwards, I had to go back to the hospital by bus.

15th of October 1944, Sunday

Mama and Fre came this afternoon. Fre had bought new clothes yesterday and looked very fine. The day after tomorrow, I will leave the hospital.

16th of October 1944

This evening we were going to the movies, when we came out of the cinema it was raining, and we got soaked. Tomorrow afternoon I will go to London.

17th of October 1944

This afternoon I was released from the hospital. I've picked up Fre from the office. It was raining terribly.

18th of October 1944

I've been to the Headquarters. I've got 4 weeks on leave. I've spent the whole day at the Headquarters. In the evening, Joop Milhado came to our house and slept there.

19th of October 1944

I went to Dunsfold. My cap was gone. My bicycle was there, but the bicycle shed, where my bike stood, was locked, and the boy who had the key had a day off. So Val, who I spoke with, will send it to me. In the afternoon I went to Guildford, and I've seen there a nice film about a man who went to Germany to find his mother, a Jewish refugee. The title of the film was 'Mr. Emanuel'. The other film was 'Hey Rookie'. Afterwards, I visited Kitty Samuels. I spend a nice evening there. Came back to London very late.

20th of October 1944

Today it's Val's birthday, 20 years. In the afternoon, I've been again at the Headquarters. I bought clothes. Went to the firm. The men gave me £ 1.15.-.[£1.30p]

21st of October 1944

Someone cheated me this morning for 18/-[90p]. In the afternoon I've been to the football with Bill and Kurt. Arsenal 0 - West Ham 3. A fantastic match, the best one that I've seen in a long time. Later we went to the city and met mama and Fre. All of us went to the movies. In the queue, there was a Dutch woman with her sister-in-law and a friend. After the film, they came with us, and we had a meal in Lyons Corner House. They invited us to come to their house tomorrow afternoon. The title of the film was 'Greenwich Village'. A wonderful film, in colors.

22nd of October 1944, Sunday

This afternoon we visited the people who I met yesterday evening. We spend there a very nice afternoon and evening.

23rd of October 1944

Lorna came to London in the morning. I've picked her up from the train. We picked up Fre, and the three of us went to Mr. Wijnberg to ask if Fre could come to cut there. He hired Fre. Afterwards, I had a meal with Lorna, and Fre went back to work. After the meal, we went dancing in the C.G.O.H. Then we drank a cup of tea, then went to the movies. 'Lost in a Harem', with Bud Abbott and Lou Costello. It was a good film. Then we went back home.

24th of October 1944

I've taken mama to the movies. 'Song of the Open Road' and 'Eternally Yours'. Both were good films in the evening to C.G.O.H. I met Violet (?). A nice girl.

27th of October 1944

In the afternoon, C.G.O.H. In the evening, Bill Boutelje and Kurt came and ate here and spent the evening with us. We played the gramophone. Tomorrow we are going to the football.

28th of October 1944

Today it's the birthday of Olive Baguley, an old girlfriend of mine. We went to the football in the afternoon, and Fre, Joyce, Bill, Kurt, Jackie, and Daantje Ritmeester came with us. Tottenham 2 - Brentford 2. It was a good match, but they played a dirty game. At 6.00 o'clock in the evening, I met Kitty Samuels, who will spend the weekend in London. First, we went to the Regent Palace, ate there and danced one dance, but it wasn't nice there, and so we went to the movies. 'Sensations 1945'. Not an interesting film. Afterwards, to Lyons to eat something. Then I brought Kitty to the house of her grandparents and came back home at...

29th of October 1944, Sunday

......1.00 o'clock this morning. At 11:30, I picked up Kitty, and she had a meal in our house together with Bill, Kurt, Jackie Ritmeester, and the two Milhado brothers, so it was very nice altogether. In the evening I've been dancing in The Royal, Tottenham. I've no problems with my leg while I'm dancing and I've to say that I feel lucky if I see all the people without legs or arms.

30th of October 1944

In the afternoon I met Kitty in the city, and we've seen a fantastic film. 'An American Romance,' with Brian Donlevy and Ann Richards. Kitty took the train to go home. I went home and went to bed at 7:30 p.m.

31st of October 1944

In the afternoon I've been dancing in the Covent Garden. In the evening, I've been to the Stage Door Canteen after I had a meal at Kahn. I met there two Dutch girls of the auxiliary corps and a Canadian paratrooper who was speaking Dutch. It was a nice evening although I don't like this place, too crowded. But the show is good.

1st of November 1944

In the afternoon I've been to the Royal, Tottenham. In the evening to the movies with mama and Fre. 'Beautiful but Broke', with Joan Davis'. 'The Hairy Ape', with William Bendix and Susan Hayward.

2nd of November 1944

I've been dancing in the afternoon in the 'Astoria'. In the evening, I visited the Kers family for half an hour.

3rd of November 1944

Today I didn't go out. In the evening, Bill and Kurt came to visit us.

4th of November 1944

In the afternoon I've been to the city for an hour together with Bill and Kurt. Then we visited Joyce, and together we went to the 21st birthday party of her friend Rosalind. It was very nice. Twenty boys and girls, all Jewish. We played fun games. We played whist until 2.00 o'clock. (Won, 7/6).[38p]

5th of November 1944 Sunday

I've been sleeping in Joyce's house and woke up at 9.00 o'clock this morning. I've been to a diamond meeting. After the meeting, I went back home. In the afternoon I've been to the movies with Bill and Kurt. In the evening, I went to Joyce's house. I've suddenly got a terrible itch; I must go to the doctor tomorrow.

6th of November 1944

I've got ointment and pills against the itch. In the evening I visit some people who used to live in Antwerp. In the evening I went to a dance for half an hour. C.G.O.H. Fre started today with work today at Wijnberg.

7th of November 1944

Lorna's birthday is today. She is 20 now. In the afternoon, I met Joan (1942). She is 23 years today. She was my girlfriend in 1942. In the afternoon, C.G.O.H. In the evening to the Royal Tottenham with Fre. Rose and Jean Wolf were also there. Met a sweet girl, Beatrice (20). Made an appointment for the coming Monday. Today I became Sergeant on the 1st of November. I had a new uniform and coat made.

8th of November 1944

I've been out with mama the whole day. First, we went to the Benavente family. Then to the old people of Bransom. Little Rita is staying there. Then I went to Camberwell to the Bransom's to pick up my civilian clothes. Then I went back home and waited for letters in the evening.

9th of November 1944

I started trying on my new suit. Then to C.G.O.H. to dance there. In the evening, Bill and Kurt came to visit us.

10th of November 1944

In the afternoon C.G.O.H. Then to the 'Stage Door Canteen'. Afterwards, I've been listening to Glenn Miller in the Queensberry Club. It was very nice. Then to Lyons.

11th of November 1944

The day of the Truce of 1914-1918. This afternoon I went to Guildford.

12th of November 1944, Sunday

I woke up at 11.00 o'clock. I had breakfast, and afterwards, I walked with Kitty. Then I had lunch, then I played cards for an hour, and at 6.00 o'clock I went to the cinema. A very bad film but I could expect it here on Sunday. At 9.20 by train back to London and came home at 12.00 o'clock.

13th of November 1944

In the afternoon, C.G.O.H. At 6 I eat at home. This evening to the Royal because I've had a date with Beatrice. We had a very nice evening. She is a good dancer. Tomorrow I will go again.

14th of November 1944

In the evening, The Royal with Fre and Beatrice. It was the final of the dancing competition last Tuesday. It was fantastic, and I had a nice evening.

15th of November 1944

In the afternoon with mama to the cinema. In the evening I stayed at home.

16th of November 1944

In the evening I've been to the Astoria to dance with Beatrice.

17th of November 1944

In the afternoon I've been to the cinema, 'Abroad with Two Yanks', with William Bendix. In the evening, Bill and Kurt came to visit us.

18th of November 1944

In the evening, I've been to a Russian ballet with mama, Fre, and Bill. It was very nice. We went to eat there altogether in a Turkish restaurant.

19th of November 1944, Sunday

This morning I've been visiting the Kersh family, J., and H. In the afternoon came Jack Mona's, a cousin of mama, to visit us, and Bill and Kurt, and at 6.00 o'clock we all together went to the movies, except Cousin Jack because he had to do 'fire watching'. A nice film, 'Gypsy Wildcat', with Maria Montez and John Hall. Afterwards, we went to eat in Lyons Strand. We met an old friend of mama, who has an orchestra there. It was a very good evening because he also played Dutch songs.

20th of November 1944

This morning I became a Sergeant officially, from the 1st of November. My leave was over, but I've got 10 days extra. Today I bought my cap and a shirt, and when I came home, I dressed immediately and I looked perfect. This evening I got a message from Maurice that he received the Flyers Cross. He really deserves it. In the evening I went to the Astoria and met Helen (23) there. I've brought her back home and made an appointment for Thursday evening.

21st of November 1944

In the afternoon, C.G.O.H. Then by train to Camberley to see Lorna. I saw her at 9.30. She didn't know that I should come so she was going to the cinema with a friend. I waited for her at the cinema, saw her for 15 minutes, we ate something and then I brought her to the billet. I had to search for a place where I could sleep, and I slept in a house of civilians.

4th of December 1944

In the afternoon I've been dancing with Max Dekker. In the evening to the Astoria with Tony (22).

5th of December 1944

In the afternoon I've been to the Astoria. In the evening, I've been to a Dutch St. Nicolaas party with mama and Fre. Nothing special.

6th of December 1944

In the afternoon I am watching 'Old Acquaintance' with Tony. A wonderful film. Bette Davis and Miriam Hopkins. Afterwards, we've been watching 'A Night in Venice'. A wonderful operetta, although I expected more from the waltzes of Strauss. It was very nice, afterwards, to Lyons. I've had a wonderful day.

7th of December 1944

In the afternoon I've been to the Astoria with Tony. In the evening with Pearl to the Astoria. We went home at 10.15 and made an appointment with Pearl for the coming Saturday. But I will not go because I must get rid of it.

8th of December 1944

This evening Albert Nabarro came to visit us and Bill, Kurt, and Joyce.

9th of December 1944

I've been to the movies with Tony in the evening. 'Casanova Crown' with Gary Cooper and Teresa Wright. Then we had a meal at 'Tavros', a Greek restaurant. I sent a telegram to Pearl in the morning that I lay in bed with a bad cold.

10th of December 1944, Sunday

Had a meal with the Kersh family. In the afternoon I've been to Tony's and went with her to the cinema. I spent the rest of the evening with her at her house.

11th of December 1944

In the evening to the movies with Pearl. Tony was also there, but downstairs, so she didn't see me. Two fantastic films. 'Ladies Courageous' with Loretta Young, and the other was 'Patrick the Great' with Donald O'Connor and Peggy Ryan.

12th of December 1944

In the evening I've been out with Tony. To the cinema 'I Love a Soldier'. Paulette Goddard and Sonny Tufs. Then to Lyons and then back home.

13th of December 1944

Today I've been the whole day to the new house. In the evening, first to C.G.O.H. Boring. Then to the Astoria. I've met there a Dutch Sergeant, Alfons de Koning. We've been drinking a beer. Before 11.00 o'clock I danced with a girl from the Ais Department, Barbara (20). I've brought her home. It was terrible foggy today.

14th of December 1944

I've been again to the house. In the evening I've been to Camberley to visit Lorna. I've slept there in the TOC. H. club. I had a bedroom there of my own. I've taken a lovely bath and had breakfast in the morning, all this for 2/6[12p]. Unbelievable cheap. / . . - . /

16th of December 1944

Today I'm 20 years old. From mama and Fre I received a nice dressing gown, from Bill £ 1. to buy a pair of gloves, from Kurt cigarettes, from Joyce an R.A.F. diary and from the lady next to us a nice black tie. From Bransom, I received 10/-[50p] to buy a shirt.

17th of December 1944, Sunday

I played football this afternoon, for the first time since I left the hospital. It wasn't bad at all; I didn't have any problem with my leg. We lost this match. Watts F.C. 2 - Bromar 0.

18th of December 1944

Today we started living in our new house in Stockwell.

19th of December 1944

In the afternoon I've been dancing in the 'Astoria'. At 6.00 o'clock I met Jan Boom. His girlfriend came with him, so the three of us went out. First, we went to a Jewish restaurant, and we had a lovely meal. Afterwards, we went dancing in the 'Astoria'. I've brought Phyllis (18) to the subway and made an appointment for this coming Thursday.

20th of December 1944

At 1.00 o'clock, Jan Boom came to us, and we had a meal together. Later we will go out with his girlfriend Audrey, Tony and I. The four of us went to the cinema. 'The Merry Monaghans, with Donald O'Connor, Peggy Ryan, and Jack Oakie. A very nice film. Afterwards, we went to Lyons and ate something there. Then we said goodbye to Jan and Audrey, and I brought Tony back home. This evening I got problems with my gums.

21st of December 1944

In the afternoon, I've been to the movies with Phyllis (18). 'Between Two Worlds', with Paul Henreid and John Garfield. A wonderful film. 'Whistling in Brooklyn', with Red Skelton. In the evening I've been to the 'Locarno' with Phyllis. A very pleasant evening. Fre received a message from Maurice that he had found his mother and sister-in-law in France.

22nd of December 1944

I've been to the dentist today. This afternoon Jan Boom came to eat with us, and then he came with me, and I bought a wonderful second-hand radio set. It costs me £ 15.-.-[75p]. So that's very cheap. I'm very happy with it.

23rd of December 1944

In the afternoon I've been to the football with Bill. Millwall 3 - Watford 3. A very good match. Millwall had bad luck because they should have won by 4 goals. In the evening I went dancing with Bill and Fre in the 'Locarno'. Phyllis went there too. She waited there for us. It was a nice evening. Jan Boon and his fiancé were also there. They were engaged yesterday.

24th of December 1944, Sunday

Today I've been to Lorna's house and spent there the whole day.

25th of December 1944

Today it's Christmas. I had a meal at Lorna's house. In the afternoon, I stayed at home, and in the evening, there was a little party at one of the sisters of Lorna's mother. We stayed there until 11.00 o'clock.

27th of December 1944

This evening I've been to the Astoria.

28th of December 1944

In the evening I've been to the Astoria. I've met Stella Sack (20).

29th of December 1944

In the afternoon I've been to the Astoria. In the evening I stayed at home.

30th of December 1944

In the afternoon I've been to the football. Crystal Palace 3 - Chelsea 3. A fantastic match. In the evening, I've been to Peckham with Fre to the Co-op. We met there Milly, Pam, Jim and his sister Pam, and Vic, all of them old friends of mine, and we had a lovely time together.

31st of December 1944, Sunday

In the afternoon I've been to the movies. In the evening, the Benavente's came to visit us. We all went together from the old year into the new year. I went to bed at 2.30 o'clock.

1st of January 1945

In the afternoon and in the evening, I've been to the Astoria. In the afternoon, I met Edith Miskin there (23), and in the evening, I took her with me back to the dance. Afterwards, we went to Lyons, and we had a meal there.

2nd of January 1945

They called me back from my leave, and I started working this morning at the Headquarters. Office work. This afternoon Maurice arrived here from Brussels. He came to eat with us in our house and after that with Max Dekker, who also did eat with us, and Fre, so the four of us, we went dancing for an hour or so. I've met Natalie (23).

3rd of January 1945

After work, I visited together with Maurice the Kersh family. We spend the whole evening there.

4th of January 1945

In the evening I am going out with Stella Sack (20). We went to the Astoria. It was very crowded there.

5th of January

From 7.45 until 7,45 tomorrow morning, I have on a watch. 24 hours. So I will stay the whole night at the Headquarters.

6th of January 1945

At 7.45, my watch was over. I went home at 1.00 o'clock. In the evening, I've been to the Balfour Club. First, we had a drink. I met Clara Miller (33) and her friend Douglas (28). Two American girls from the Army. We made an appointment for coming Tuesday, but probably we are not going. Back in the Club, I met Pearl (21), and afterwards, she came with us to Lyons to eat something.

8th of January 1945

In the evening, I've been out with Dorothy and Marie Holding. We were with the four of us. I've made an appointment with Dorothy for coming Thursday, but I won't go. I'll send her a telegram.

9th of January 1945

I stayed at home in the evening. I didn't go to the American girls.

10th of January 1945

In the evening I've been to the 'Locarno' with Maurice. I met Edith Miller there (25). Maurice with Edith's friend Kay. Nice evening.

11th of January 1945

First, I've been to the movies with Maurice. '30 seconds over Tokyo'. A nice film over the Mitchells. After that, I've been to the Astoria. I met there Milly (19) and Ray Moscow. I've had a good evening. Also, Stella Sack was there with her sister Ann, and both walked with us when we went back home.

12th of January 1945

I stayed at home. Bill Boutelje came to visit us.

13th of January 1945

In the afternoon I've been to the movies. 'Bathing Beauty', with Red Skelton and Esther Williams. It was really a fantastic film. In the evening to the 'Locarno'. Have I met Mrs. Irene Kay? A very nice person. I brought her back home after the dance.

14th of January 1945, Sunday

In the afternoon, Joyce came, and she ate with us. Maurice and I went to the Netherlands House. I met there Renee Levy (18), and Maurice met a girl. The four of us had been drinking tea together. In the evening, I've been to a Jewish Organisation. They are much nicer people than who we normally meet. The name of the club is 'Young Israel'. We had a wonderful evening. I met Beryl Eagles (20). A very nice girl. After the dance, I brought her to the underground

15th of January 1945

In the evening I've been to the 'Locarno', with Maurice. We met there Pat (21), and Lilian 26) and walked a while with them.

16th of January 1945

In the evening to the 'Locarno'. Kay and Edith were also there because we had an appointment with them. It wasn't very nice.

17th of January 1945

In the morning I've been to the dentist. After that, I picked up Beryl (20), and we had dinner together. Then I went back to the Headquarters. When I came back, there was a message from Mr. Boom that I had to call him. So I called him, and he told me to come to his wedding and that he had already booked rooms.

18th of January 1945

Today I have been on watch. At 5.00 o'clock it's finished, but on Saturday I will be on watch from in the morning at 9.30 until Sunday morning at 9.30. In the evening I went to the 'Astoria'. I met you there at Hilda Wine garden (21). After the dance, I brought her to the underground.

21st of January 1945, Sunday

At 9.30, the watch finished. Mama has become 57 years today. At 6.00 o'clock I went by train to Bradford to attend tomorrow the wedding of Jaap Boom, my navigator. I arrived at 12.00 o'clock. The boom was already waiting for me. He brought me to the hotel where I stayed overnight.

22nd of January 1945

The wedding was at 2.30 in the afternoon. Afterwards, there was a reception. I've written a little poem, and I was reading that. I had written it on a piece of cardboard. The bride, Rita Fowler, liked it so much that she wanted to keep it as a souvenir. On the backside of the cardboard, there was written a warning to be careful with water. To be conserved with it. It was laying in my room. First, I was introduced by the Best Man, the pilot, Ryan Collee. He said that everybody was so happy to see me after being released from the hospital, after being wounded in action. A lot of applause, etc. .... I bought a very nice present, a silver-plated nutcracker, very heavy. The bride and groom were very happy with this present. I met there a W.A.A.F. girl, Joyce Little (22). A very nice girl. After the reception, we went to the house of the Foley family, and we stayed there until 12.00 o'clock. I've given a picture to the family and promised to write them regularly. I will also write to Joyce when she must go back father her leave.

23rd of January 1945

I left Bradford at 7.25. I had bought a newspaper at the station, and the picture of the wedding was placed in the newspaper already. I will keep it with me. It's a nice memory of the pleasant time I had in Bradford. I arrived in London at 2.00 o'clock. Arrived at the Headquarters at 2.30. Worked there until 5.00 o'clock. After that, I met Beryl Eagles (20), and we went together to the cinema. 'Frenchmen's Creek', a very nice film, with Joan Fontaine. Then we had a meal in the Piccadilly Brasserie. Very good there. At 10.15, we both went back home. I arrived home at 10.45 p.m. Maurice arrived just after me, and he told me that he and Joyce Kersh had decided to get married. I don't want to say one word about it. Tomorrow Helen will be getting married. I've made a speech for the bride and groom, maybe Maurice will read it. I can't be there before 5.45 p.m. also I made a little poem.

24th of January 1945

I've been to the wedding. It was terribly crowded. I've sung there, 'So Deep is the Night' and 'I'll Walk Alone'. I made an appointment with Milly Perlow (19) to go dancing in the 'Astoria' coming Monday. First, I've asked permission from her coming parents-in-law, aunt Minnie, and Uncle Harry. They agreed.

25th and 26th of January 1945

In the evening I stayed at home.

27th of January 1945

Bill and Kurt came to visit us in the afternoon. In the evening to Maccabi. A Jewish organisation. It wasn't very nice. When I went back home, I met two girls in the subway who also had been there. One of them asked me to come to a little party in Forest Gate coming Sunday. I accepted the offer.

28th of January 1945, Sunday

I visited the Bransom family this afternoon. Then I met Joyce and Maurice. The three of us went to Roseke, a Belgian restaurant, and had a meal there and then we went dancing at 'Young Israel'. Beryl was also there. I met there Sabine ((21), a girl from Antwerp. We brought her and her friends to the tube.

30th of January 1945

I've heard this afternoon that Elias Zomerplaag has arrived in London from Indië. I've written him already so he can come to us as soon as possible. In the evening I've been to the 'Locarno' with Maurice. I met Winnie Baker (23). Made an appointment for the coming Monday.

31st of January 1945

In the afternoon, I've been to a funeral of a Dutch officer from the Navy. In the evening I've been to the movies with Fre and Maurice. Not a good film. 'Western Approaches'. The first film was much nicer. 'Lady Let's Dance', with Delita.

1st of February 1945

Today I had to watch.

2nd of February 1945

This evening I stayed at home and went to bed at 10.00 o'clock. The whole evening I listened to the radio.

3rd of February 1945

Elias Zomerplaag came to visit us. In the afternoon we've been to the 'Locarno'. With Maurice and Elias. Maurice visited in the evening Kersh family and Elias, and I went to the 'Locarno' again.

4th of February 1945 Sunday

In the morning, I walked with Maurice. In the afternoon, I've been to a little party for Jewish girls and boys. I've had a wonderful day. I left at 9.15. We were with 8 people. I brought Helen Lubel (19) partially to her home by tube.

5th of February 1945

I've been dancing in the 'Locarno' with Winnie Baker (23). Maurice also came, although he isn't living with us anymore since yesterday. He took part in a nice competition, and I laughed a lot. He came second.

6th of February 1945

First to the cinema. 'Up in Arms'. A fantastic film, with Danny Kaye and Dinah Shore. After that, I went dancing in the 'Astoria'. I met Margaret Carroll there (25). I brought her home and made an appointment for the coming Thursday.

7th of February 1945

To the 'Locarno' with Maurice and Elias. I met Sheila (17) and brought her back home after the dance.

8th of February 1945

I've got a paste. It never happens. So I went dancing in 'Covent Garden'. There was a competition. I took part in it with a girl that I met there. Cris Gregory (23). She was a good dancer. We came until the final and became third. Sixteen couples took part. The first prize was £ 1.10.[£1.50p]-. and the second prize was £1.-.-. Each of us. By mistake they gave me the £ 1.10.-. And, of course, I didn't bring it back. It was a nice evening. I think there were 2.000 people. After the dance, we took a drink and then we went to eat something and then I brought Cris to the tube.

10th of February 1945

This afternoon I've been to the football with Maurice. Millwall 3 - Brentford 2. A good match. Bad weather. After the football, we went by bus to the City to meet there Sabine (21) and Helen (19). The four of us went to the cinema. 'Bowery to Broadway'. With Maria Montez and Jack Oakie. Then we had a lovely meal in Lyons Corner House. I brought Helen back home.

11th of February 1945, Sunday

First, in the morning, I've been to Mrs. Bransom. I gave her a little present because it's her birthday today. Then I met Maurice. Went to the cinema. 'Winged Victory'. Then we had a meal. At 7.30 I met Sabine, and we went to 'Maccabi', met there Helen. There was a talent competition. It was very good. After that, there was a final ping pong. Brought Helen back home.

12th of February 1945

At 12.30 in the afternoon, I had lunch with Helen. In the evening I've been dancing with Fre and Maurice in the 'Paramount'. There is nothing special there, but one band is fantastic. I met Margaret Holmes (22). I brought her back home after we brought Fre to the tube.

13th of February 1945

I went to the cinema at 5.30. The Marx Brothers in 'A Night at the Opera'. At 8.15 I met Margaret, and we went to the Piccadilly Brasserie' to eat and dance. It was nice but very expensive.

14th of February 1945

I had lunch with Maurice and Helen. In the evening I've been to a nice show with mama and Fre. 'Strike it Again' with Sid Field. A good show. On our way home, we took a W.R.E.N. on the way to put her on the right bus.

15th of February 1945

In the afternoon I had lunch with Helen. In the evening I've been dancing in the 'Astoria'. I met there an old girlfriend, Florrie (21), and after the dance, I brought her back home.

17th of February 1945

In the afternoon to the 'Locarno' with Maurice. I met Kathleen there (23). In the evening I've been out with Maurice and Helen, we went to the movies. 'The Woman in the Window', with Joan Bennett and Edward G. Robinson. Not a special film. Then we had a meal, and then I brought Helen back home.

18th of February 1945, Sunday

In the afternoon with Maurice to the Netherlands House. Hopeless again. Then we had a meal. Then to 'Maccabi'. Met Helen there. Afterwards, I've brought her to the train.

19th of February 1945

In the afternoon I had lunch with Helen. In the evening with Maurice and Phyllis (18) to the 'Locarno'. Phyllis and I took part in a competition where we had to dance 16 different dances. We won the first prize. Phyllis received a handbag, and I got a leather pouch to put in hairbrushes, combs, etc., for travelling.

20th of February 1945

With Maurice, his A.T.S. girl and her friend we went dancing in 'Covent Garden'. We had a misunderstanding. In the afternoon I had lunch with Helen.

22nd of February 1945

I stayed at home in the evening.

23rd of February 1945

I stayed at home in the evening. Bill and Kurt came to visit us.

24th of February 1945

At 12.55, just before I left the office, I read on tasks that I would be transferred. Came home with Helen, and she ate with us. Mama is in a terrible bad mood. All the time, she cried. After the meal at the football, Millwall 1 - Fulham 0. A good match. Then back home. First, we had to eat and then I brought with Helen to the cinema. 'Meet me in St. Louis'. A coloured film with Judy Garland and a 7-years old girl, a new little movie star, Margaret O'Brien. Then we went to Lyons. Helen stayed with us overnight.

25th of February 1945, Sunday

This morning I've been visiting the Bransom family, together with Helen. At 2.30 in the afternoon we met Maurice and Sabine, the four of us went to Helen's house, and I met for the first time her parents. We had there a cup of tea. After that, we went to the city and to the cinema. 'None but the Lonely Heart', with Cary Grant and June Duprez. A sad film, but they played wonderfully. Then we went to Lyons Corner House to eat something. Then I brought Helen back home.

26th of February 1945

In the morning, I've been to Mr. Zoethout. He told me that the transfer was a mistake. At 12.30 I had lunch with mama and Helen. At 5.00 o'clock Elias Zomerplaag went with me to our house. We ate at home and then we danced in the 'Hammersmith'. I met Susan (24). A nice girl. She brought me to the train.

27th of February 1945

Stayed at home in the evening. Helen ate with us and stayed overnight.

28th of February 1945

In the evening, I visit the Kersh family.

6th of March 1945

I had lunch with Helen in the afternoon. In the evening she eats with us at our house. Afterwards, I've been to Empress Brixton with Helen and Fre to watch a show. Helen did sleep in our house.

7th of March 1945

In the morning, I went with Helen to the office. She works around the corner there. In the evening I was at Helen's house, had a meal there and spent the whole evening there. At 11.00 o'clock I went back home again.

8th of March 1945

In the afternoon I had lunch with Helen. In the evening I've been to a W.R.E.N. dance with Elias Zomerplaag. Left there at 10.30. I didn't like it at all.

9th of March 1945

At 12.30 I went for a walk with Helen in Hyde Park. Maurice and his girlfriend were also with us. In the evening I stayed at home. Bill, Mrs. Benavente, and Elias have eaten with us. After the meal, the son of Mrs. Benavente came also, and we played cards.

10th of March 1945

Today I stay at watch. In the afternoon, I've been to Harrow by car. Almost the whole way back, I drove the car myself. In the evening, Helen and Fre came for a little while to see me.

11th of March 1945 Sunday

Helen came to our house and did eat something. Then we went for a visit to the Benavente family. Then we went to the city. To the cinema. 'Tonight and Every Night'. A coloured film with Rita

Hayworth, Lee Bowman, and Janet Blair. A very nice film. Afterwards to Lyons Corner House for a lovely meal, and then I brought Helen back home.

12th of March 1945

I had lunch with Helen in the afternoon. In the evening, she eats with us. Also, Elias came. Then the three of us went to the movies. 'The Man of Half Moon Street'. A very nice film. 'San Diagonal I Love You' was the other film and was also a very nice film. The movie stars were Jon Hall and Louise Albritton. Helen stayed with us overnight.

13th of March 1945

Together with Helen, I went to the office this morning. At 12.30 I had a new suit fitted. Then I had something to eat with Helen. In the evening, we visited the Kersh family and the Haring family.

14th of March 1945

At 6.00 o'clock I went with Helen to her house. We ate there and then we went to the cinema. 'Kipps' with Phyllis Calvert and Michael

Redgrave. 'Practically Yours' with Claudette Colbert and Fred Mac Murray. Then back home. I've been sleeping at Helen's house.

15th of March 1945

Together with Helen, I went to the office. At 12.30 we had lunch together. In the evening I stayed at home.

16th of March 1945

I stayed at home this evening. Jaak Grunblatt and Elias came for a visit.

18th of March 1945 Sunday

In the morning, I went for a drive with Helen. I already woke up with a stiff neck. We went to Richmond. We arrived back at Helen's house at 5.45. I took a bath. Then I dressed up, and we went to an engagement party. I didn't feel well, and everything was painful. Stayed and slept at Helen's house.

19th of March 1945

I felt a little bit better this morning. Went together with Helen to the office. I've been to see the doctor, but he even didn't want to look at me. At 12.30 I went for lunch with Helen. In the evening, she came to us and stayed to eat. Afterwards, we went to visit Mina Wyatt, the sister of Mrs. Bransom. At 10.00 o'clock we went back home. Helen slept here.

20th of March 1945

Together we went this morning to the office. At 12.30 I played football in Hyde Park with the boys from the Headquarters. In the evening, I visit the Kersh family together with mama.

21st of March 1945

Today it's Spring. A beautiful day. At 12.30 I played football again. I played as a goalkeeper. We won 1-0. In the evening I went out with Maurice. Tomorrow he will go back to the continent.

22nd of March 1945

Today I must watch. In the evening, Helen came to see me. Stayed until 8.00 o'clock.

23rd of March 1945

At 12.30 I played football again. I played as a goalkeeper. We won 4-2. Elias, Bill, and Kurt came in the evening for a visit.

24th of March 1945

In the afternoon Helen came to our house. We didn't go out. Also, in the evening, we stayed at home. Helen slept here.

25th of March 1945 Sunday

In the afternoon we were going to a wedding of very good friends of the Lubel family. It was a nice reception. There was a dance band, and the whole afternoon people were dancing. In the evening, Helen didn't feel well, and we stayed at home. At 11, I left and went back home.

26th of March 1945

In the evening, I went to the operetta 'Gay Rosalinde', derived from 'Die Fledermaus'. Mama and Fre came with me also. I should like to see this operetta again.

27th of March 1945

In the evening I've been dancing in the 'Astoria' with Max Dekker. In the afternoon I played football as a goalkeeper. We lost 2-1.

28th of March 1945

First evening Jomtof. Stayed at home. Max Dekker came for a visit.

30th of March 1945

For the first time since mama and Fre were here, I went out on Friday evening. I went to the 'Locarno' with Elie. I've met Connie Darke (19). Brought her to the subway. (W.R.E.N.).

31st of March 1945

I've got a day off today. I travelled to Bognor with Helen to spent there the holiday days (3). I met there a couple of Jewish people there, and we also stayed there with Jewish people who were very nice to us. In the evening we all went together to the pub. Afterwards, we went to one of the houses of one of those families, and we played cards there until 1.30 a.m.

1st of April 1945 (First day of Easter)

We slept until 2.00 o'clock. After lunch, I went to the cinema with Helen and the son of the family where we stayed. 'Mr. Big' with Donald O'Connor and Peggy Ryan. The other film was 'Sanders of the Rivers' with Paul Robeson and Leslie Banks. Two good films. Then back to Middleton by bus. In the evening we went to visit other people with Bob and Tonie, and we played cards until...

2nd of April 1945 (Second day of Easter)

....5.00 o'clock this morning. We came back at 5.30 and had a meal before we went to bed. It was 6.30 when we lay in bed. We slept till1.00 o'clock. After lunch, we have been walking to the sea. Then we went to the house of Bob and Tonie, we got people for a visit and played cards again until 7.30. We went back to London by train at 8.45. Tomorrow I will have the watch. Otherwise, we could have stayed another night in Bogor. I arrived home at 12.00 o'clock.

3rd of April 1945

Today I had to watch. It's hopeless. In the evening I played cards for an hour, and I won £ 1.3.[£1'15p]-. That's good to put it with the money for my new uniform.

4th of April 1945

This morning I went quickly to Helen's house and had breakfast there. In the afternoon I played football in Hyde Park. I was the goalkeeper. The result was 1-1. In the evening Helen came to our house and did eat with us. Went to the 'Empress'.

5th of April 1945

In the afternoon I played football again. 1-1. In the evening, I went for an hour to drink with the boys from the Fly Service.

6th of April 1945

In the afternoon, I picked up my new uniform. It fits me fantastic. In the evening I stayed at home.

7th of April 1945

In the afternoon, I went to the Cup Final with Helen, Bill, and Kurt. Millwall 0 - Chelsea 2. Not a good match. Then we had a meal in the city and then to the cinema. 'Keep Your Powder Dry' with Lana Turner, Lorraine Day, and Susan Peters.

8th of April 1945 Sunday

In the morning, I visited the Bransom family. In the afternoon Rom Moas and cousin Jaak came for a visit. Also came the mother of Ada, who was in Germany together with Fre. In the evening I've been to the movies with Helen. 'Stage Door Canteen'. It's for the second time that I have seen this film. Afterwards, to Lyons to eat something.

10th of April 1945

I played football in the afternoon. We lost, 2-0. I've put together a team to play a match tomorrow against a Dutch army team. In the evening I've been to the Stage Door Canteen. I met there two friends of mine. One was Eddie, a Jewish boy, also an air gunner, who was together with me in Lasham and Finmere. The other one was Paddy, a boy who was at the same time as me in the hospital in Halton. I've met Doris Rawson (21) (A.T.S.). Nice girl.

11th of April 1945

At 12.30 in the afternoon, I trained for this evening. We won 4-1. On the evening of the match. Navy Headquarters 8 - Dutch Army 0. I scored twice, and I've given several passes. We had a little accident with a stupid woman. After the match, I went with Elie to the 'Stage Door Canteen'.

12th of April 1945

This afternoon I've been playing football again. We won, 2-0. In the evening I stayed at home.

13th of April 1945

In the morning, I was inspected. At 12.30 I made a walk with Helen. (Yesterday we had a fight and today it's still not good between us). In the evening I stayed at home. Bill, Kurt, and Elie came for a visit.

14th of April 1945

Helen came in the afternoon. Everything is okay again, in the evening we went to the cinema. 'The Unseen' with Joe Mac. Crea and Gail Russell. A nice film. Then we ate and then I brought Helen back home.

15th of April 1945, Sunday

Today I have to watch. It's a pity because the weather is beautiful.

16th of April 1945

I played football in the afternoon. Five people against twelve. It's a bit crazy. We lost just 1-0. In the evening, I visited the Bransom family. I met Dick Edwards, my best friend, in 1942, before I went into the army. He also became an air gunner a short time ago. I have been drinking a beer with him.

17th of April 1945

In the afternoon I played football. We lost with 4-3. The weather has been beautiful since last Friday. It's too hot to play football. In the evening, I went out with Doris Rawson. First to the movies. Bud Abbott and Lou Costello in 'Here Come the Co-Ed's'. Nothing special. Then I went to Ealing to bring Doris back home. I missed the train to go back, 10 seconds late. I got lucky. I got a free ride to Victoria. Then I took a taxi to go home. I went for a short visit to the Benavente family because they expected their son to come. I stayed there until...

18th of April 1945

...1.00 o'clock this morning. Then I went home. In the evening I was lying in Hyde Park from 5.00 until 7.00. Helen came at 6.00 o'clock. We had a meal. Then we went to her house. Again we had a meal. I slept in Helen's house.

19th of April 1945

I went to the office together with Helen. In the evening I stayed at home. Jaak and Celia Grunblatt came for a visit. Elie came also.

22nd of April 1945, Sunday

At 12.00 o'clock I went to Helen's house. I spent there the whole day and stayed there to sleep.

23rd of April 1945

In the morning we went together to the office. At 12.30 I played football. We won 3-1. In the evening we went dancing in the 'Locarno'. It was very nice.

24th of April 1945

In the afternoon I played football. 1-1. Helen came in the evening. And Ro Mona's and the Benavente family. We had a nice talk the whole evening.

25th of April 1945

I bought for £1 a pair of second-hand football shoes. In the afternoon I played football. We won 2-0. I scored once. In the evening I went with Helen to a football match. R. Norwegian N. - R. Netherlands Navy 0-7. Then to Helen's house. Stayed there overnight.

26th of April 1945

In the afternoon I played football. We won 4-2. I've made one goal. In the evening I went out with Connie Darke. (19) (W.R.E.N.). First, we did eat something, then went to the movies. 'Blithe Spirit'. After that, we had something to eat again. I didn't go home but stayed overnight in a Forces club.

27th of April 1945

Today I had the watch. In the morning, I went with a sergeant to the police station to help translate in a case of theft. In the evening C. came from 7.00-11.00. Helen called me while C. was with me. I had a very uncomfortable feeling.

28th of April 1945

Helen came to eat with us. Then we went to the football. Millwall 4 - Clapton Or. 1. A good match. Then to the cinema. Fre also came with us. 'A Guest in the House' with Ann Baxter, Ralph Bellamy. She Gets her Man' with Joan Davis. Afterwards, we went dancing in the Co-op Peckham. I met a lot of old friends and girlfriends of mine. A nice evening. Afterwards walked. Milly, my ex-girlfriend who still is a singer in the band, came with us back. It was pouring rain, and we became soaking wet.

29th of April 1945, Sunday

In the afternoon I went to the movies with Jack Grunblatt, his wife and Helen. 'Lido to Mystery' with William Cargan and Margaret Lindsay. 'Reveille with Beverley' with Ann Miller. Then we went to the Bransom family and had a cup of tea there. Then Mr. Bransom came back with us to visit the Grunblatt family, and we played cards until 10.30 o'clock. Afterwards, I brought Helen to Waterloo, and I went home.

30th of April 1945

At 6.15, I went to Chatham. I arrived there at 7.35. Went to the movies. 'The Man from Morocco' with Anton Walbrook and Martha Scott. I stayed overnight in Chatham.

1st of May 1945

I got out of my bed at 6.30. I arrived back in London at 8.20. I had breakfast in Lyons. I was back on time at the Headquarters. At 12.30 I had lunch with Helen. In the evening to the Co-op. I brought Milly back home.

2nd of May 1945

In the afternoon I played football. We won 2-1. I made the two goals. In the evening with the four of us to the movies. Including Elie Zomerplaag. The title of the film was 'Laura' with Gene Tierney. Connie had to go back to her camp, so I brought her to the train.

3rd of May 1945

In the morning, I had to go to court for another case. This time the boy of the Navy was guilty, but I talked until I got him out. Very interesting. In the evening to an A.T.S. dance with Elie.

4th of May 1945

In the evening I stayed at home. Good news on the radio. In Italy, 1.000.000 men surrendered.

5th of May 1945

In the afternoon to the movies with Helen. In the evening to the Netherlands House. I met Fre there.

6th of May 1945 Sunday

I spend the whole day in Southend with Fre, Helen, Bill, and Kurt. It was a nice day.

7th of May 1945

In the afternoon I played football. We lost 1-0. A good match. Today the war is over. In the evening came, Jack and Celia Grunblatt to visit us. We played cards until 11.00 o'clock. Then we had a nice time at the 'Bonfire'. At 12.00 o'clock, we picked up Pop Benavente, and we played cards with the Grunblatt family until 3.00 o'clock in the morning.

8th of May 1945

V.E. Day

At 11.00 o'clock, I was already drunk at the Headquarters. I went drinking with Jacobs and Van de Velde. Afterwards, I didn't feel good, and they brought me to a hotel. I woke up at 7.30 in the evening. I washed myself and dressed up. Then I went for a walk. I also went to the Netherlands House. I came back home at 1.30 in the morning. The whole evening I had been walking.

9th of May 1945

This morning Bill and Kurt came to visit us. In the afternoon I went out with Helen. We went walking in Regents Park. Afterwards, we drank a cup of tea in the Cumberland Hotel. Then to the Netherlands House. We had dinner there. After that, we went walking. I've seen a lot of Dutch people. Had a lot of fun. Everything in the city looks crazy. In the evening, I slept at Helen's house.

11th of May 1945

I went to the office by bike. In the afternoon I played football. We won 3-0. I made one goal. Today it's terribly hot. Much too hot to play football. In the evening I stayed at home. Elie came to visit us. Went for a walk for an hour.

12th of May 1945

I went to the office together with Helen. Five years ago, the war started.

12th of May 1945

In the afternoon I went home with Helen. In the evening with her and her sister to the cinema. Later her mother came also. 'Here Comes the Waves', with Betty Hutton, Bing Crosby, and Sonny Tufts. I stayed at Helen's house to sleep.

13th of May 1945 Sunday

Today 5 years ago, I left my house when the war was going on for three days. Early in the morning, I went to Westcliff-on-Sea with Helen. During the whole morning, we had beautiful weather. In the afternoon, it became terrible windy. Mama and Fre did also come, and we met them there. We also met Jean and Harry, two people from London. Coming Thursday, we will go out with them. We were back at Helen's house at 11.00 o'clock, and I stayed there to sleep.

14th of May 1945

In the morning, I went to the office together with Helen. In the afternoon I played football. Very windy. We lost 2-1. I made the only goal. A nice goal. For a change, I went dancing in the evening in the 'Astoria'. I met there Camille Hofmann (28), a girl from Czech girl who had a relationship with one of our officers long ago. After the dance, I walked with her to her house.

15th of May 1945

This afternoon I played football. We won 3-0. I made all three goals. (The fourth was disallowed). A good match. In the evening, I went with mama to the Empress Brixton theatre. A nice show.

16th of May 1945

In the afternoon I played football. We won 4-1. I made two goals. In the evening I went to the Stage Door Canteen. It was a good show.

17th of May 1945

In the afternoon I played football. We won 1-0. In the evening I went out with Helen, Harry, and Jean, the people who we met last Sunday. We went to a dinner dance in the Regents Palace.

18th of May 1945

In the afternoon I played football. We won 1-0. In the evening I stayed at home. Got a visit from Bill, Kurt, and Elie.

19th of May 1945

First, at 1.00 o'clock I had a meal with Helen in a kosher restaurant. Afterwards to the football. Tottenham-Arsenal 4-0. Then we ate and then went to the cinema. 'Medal for Bennie'. Dorothy

Lamour and John Nash. A bad film. Afterwards, I brought Helen to her house.

20th of May 1945, Sunday

In the afternoon I stayed at Helen's place. At 6.00 o'clock with her, her parents and her sister Joan to the cinema. 'Mr. Lucky' with John Wayne and Claire Trevor. A good film.

21st of May 1945 Pentecost

Today I have a day off. In the afternoon I went to Helen's house. First, we went in the evening to the cinema. Then it started raining. I wore my civil suit and got soaking wet. We went to Golders Green 'Hippodrome'. It was very nice. Harry Roy and his band.

22nd of May 1945

In the afternoon I played football. We won 4-1. In the evening, Dick Edwards came to eat with us.

24th of May 1945

At 5.00 o'clock I went to the Stage Door Canteen for an hour, because we ate quite late. Helen came to eat with us. Afterwards, we went with the four of us to the Brixton Empress. It was a very nice show. Helen slept with us.

25th of May 1945

In the morning, I went with Helen to the office. In the afternoon I played football. 1-1. In the evening, I went to the Netherlands House with Elie and Dick Edwards. I had a nice evening.

26th of May 1945

At 1.00 o'clock I went with Helen to Bognor. We spend the weekend with her sister and brother-in-law. A lot of friends came in the evening.

27th of May 1945 Sunday

Today the weather is beautiful. In the evening the four of us went to the cinema. 'Treat em rough' with Peggy Moran and Eddie Albert. 'Millions like us', a fantastic film.

28th of May 1945

Early in the morning, we came back. I start working for Mr. Kosten. First thing in the afternoon, I went to the dentist. Then I went to dinner with Cor Schot, who just came back from captivity, and his wife, Edna. At 9.00 o'clock in the evening, I went to bed.

29th of May 1945

In the afternoon I played football. We lost 1-0. In the evening I went dancing in the 'Astoria'. I've met Guthrie (20).

30th of May 1945

In the afternoon I played football. We won 2-0. I made both goals. In the evening I went to the cinema with Helen. 'For you Alone' with all English movie stars. 'Under the Clock' with Judy Garland and Robert Walker. A fantastic film. I slept at Helen's place.

1st of June 1945

At 12.30 I went for lunch with Helen and Max Dekker. This morning I've been transferred from the Headquarters to Park Lane. During the transfer, I lost my pair of hand gloves. In the evening I stayed at home. I must work now until 6.00 o'clock.

2nd of June 1945

In the afternoon I went to the football. Chelsea 1 - Bolton W. 2. A good match. After that, I met Helen. Then to the movies. 'Hollywood Canteen' is a very nice film. Then we went to dinner, went with Helen to her house and slept there.

3rd of June 1945 Sunday

Helen came with me to our house. The whole day people came to visit us. At 7.30 in the evening, we went to 'Maccabi' for an hour. Brought Helen back home.

4th of June 1945

This afternoon I went again to the dentist. I had to have a tooth filled again. In the evening for an hour to the 'Brixton Empress'. A good show.

7th of June 1945

Mr. and Mrs. Lubel have been married for 25 years today. I've given them a nice silver-plated dish to put a cake on. In the evening I went with them, their daughter and Helen, to a nice show. 'The Night and the Music'.

8th of June 1945

In the evening I stayed at home. We got a visit from the Grunblatt family.

9th of June 1945

In the afternoon, I went to visit the Bransom family with Fre. In the evening I went to the cinema with Helen. 'Carolina Blues' with

Ann Miller and Kay Keizer and his band. 'Sudan' with Maria Montez, John Hall, and Turban Bay.

10th of June 1945, Sunday

This morning I went to the shul with Helen because a friend of hers got married. In the afternoon we stayed at home until 6.30 and then we went to the reception. We've had the honour to sit at the same table with the bride and groom and with the best man and his wife. Also, we've got an invitation to come for a visit to the best man and his wife. The groom is also working in the diamond business, and he will look to get me a ring for my engagement in August.

11th of June 1945

In the evening, I went with Helen to the 'Brixton Empress'. Not as good as usual.

12th of June 1945

Today I've got my last two vaccines in case I should go to the Netherlands on leave. I feel terrible and miserable. Mama, Fre, and I went to the Lubel family and did eat there. At 10.00 o'clock we went back home.

13th of June 1945

The whole day I felt the pain of the vaccination. In the evening I felt a little bit better. We went for a visit to Jerry and Marianne, the people who we met last Sunday. A beautiful place, the food was delicious, and the whole evening we played cards. At 11.00 o'clock they brought us by car back to Helen's place. I slept there.

14th of June 1945

In the afternoon I played football. We won 4-1. I made two goals. In the evening to the 'Stage Door Canteen'. I've met Pamela Thornton (20). A W.A.A.F.

15th of June 1945

In the afternoon I played football. We won by 3-2. I made one goal. In the evening we've got people who visited us.

16th of June 1945

I went out with Elie.

17th of June 1945, Sunday

Today I have to watch. The weather is beautiful, so my weekend is hopeless.

18th of June 1945

In the afternoon I played football. 1-1. In the evening I stayed at home.

20th of June 1945

In the evening Helen and I went again to visit Jerry and Marianne because they had invited us again. It was a pleasant evening again.

21st of June 1945

Today the Summer has begun. I went to bed at 7.30 in the evening.

22nd of June 1945

In the afternoon I played football. We won 3-1. I made a goal. In the evening I went with Fre to the Netherlands House. It wasn't nice at all.

23rd of June 1945

In the evening, I went out with Beattie and her fiancé to a dinner dance in the Trocadero. We had a nice evening and had a good time.

24th of June 1945

With the six of us, we went swimming in the Finchley swimming pool. In the evening we went to visit Beattie, who was also with us, and we had a nice evening. At 10.30 I put Fre on the train, and I went with Helen to her place and slept there.

25th of June 1945

For a change, I went in the evening to the 'Covent Garden' for dancing. I met there a nice girl, Ju. Jones (18) and talked with her the whole evening.

26th of June 1945

In the afternoon I played football. We won 3-1. I made all three goals. In the evening I was with Helen because she didn't feel good.

27th of June 1945

In the afternoon I played football. We lost with 9-4. A heavy defeat, and we don't lose often. In the evening I stayed at home.

28th of June 1945

In the evening I went dancing in the 'Astoria'.   J.J. Ring. £54

29th of June 1945

Today I had to watch.

30th of June 1945

At 11.18, I took the train to Bognor with Helen. The whole day it was bad weather, so we didn't go out.

1st of July 1945

Because today the weather is too bad, we didn't go out again, so we could have spent our time better in London.

2nd of July 1945

We all overslept this morning. I came to my work more than an hour late.

3rd of July 1945

In the afternoon I played football. We played 2-2. I made one goal in the evening to go to the cinema. 'To Have and Have not', with Humphrey Bogart and Lauren Bacall.

4th of July 1945

In the evening, I went to the Brixton Empress. A nice show.

5th of July 1945

In the afternoon I played football. We lost 4-1. I made the one and only goal. In the evening I went with Helen to the cinema. 'They were Sisters', with Phyllis Calvert. I slept at Helen's place.

6th of July 1945

In the afternoon I played football. I was the goalkeeper. We won 3-2. In the evening I went out with Maurice, who has been here for 2 days. We went to the Stage Door Canteen.

7th of July 1945

In the afternoon and the evening, I went out with Maurice and Fre. First, we went to the movies. 'The Fifth Chair', afterwards we danced in the 'Locarno'. Helen went today for a holiday in Bournemouth.

8th of July 1945 Sunday

In the afternoon, I went with Maurice to the Netherlands House. In the evening to the 'Locarno'.

9th of July 1945

In the afternoon I played football. We played 2-2. Make one goal in the evening to the cinema. 'Tomorrow the World', with Betty Field, Friedrich March, and a new, 12- or 13 years old movie star Skippy Homeijer.

10th of July 1945

I went to Millwall, and they gave me a massage there. No training because the weather was too bad. In the evening, I visited the Grunblatt family.

11th of July 1945

Today I had to watch.

12th of July 1945

In the afternoon I played football. We lost 4-1. In the evening to the Stage Door Canteen. Pam Thornton. Nice show. Dor. Rawson (18th of April) was there too. Very mad.

13th of July 1945

I was in a bad mood. I went away in the evening. Stage Door Canteen. Rawson was also there. I brought her back home.

14th of July 1945

In the afternoon I went for an hour to the cinema. 'Bring on the Girls', with Veronica Lake, Sonny Tufts, and Eddie Bracken. Then I went to the house of Helen and waited there for her because she had come back from Bournemouth. At 6.00 o'clock she came home. Late in the evening, we made a walk and visited the De Wilde family.

16th of July 1945

In the evening to the 'Locarno'. I met there Nancy Weads (20), an Ensa girl, and her friend. Within a few weeks, they are going to India to dance there for the troops. After the dance, I brought them to the train.

17th of July 1945

I received today a present from Helen. A wonderful clothes brush with a leather handle. In the evening I played football. A heavy training, but okay. Afterwards, I met N., and we went to the movies. 'Experiment Perilous', with Hedy Lamar, Paul Lucas, and George Brent.

18th of July 1945

First, I went in the evening to the Stage Door Canteen for an hour. After that, I met D. Rawson. We went to the 'Hammersmith Palais de Dance' for dancing. I've brought D. back home.

19th of July 1945

In the afternoon, I went for lunch with N. In the evening to the cinema with Helen. 'Diamond Horseshoe' with Betty Grable, Phil Silvers, and Dick Haymes. A nice film. Afterwards, we went to Lyons to eat something and then with Helen to her house. I slept there.

20th of July 1945

We went together to the office this morning. In the evening, Helen came with me to our house. She wasn't in our house for about 2 months. She slept here.

21st of July 1945

Together we went to the office this morning.

22nd of July 1945, Sunday

First thing in the afternoon we went to the 'Netherlands House'. In the evening we went to Helen's house. At 11.00 o'clock I went back home.

23rd of July 1945

Today I watched. Helen came to visit me for an hour in the evening.

24th of July 1945

Early in the morning, I left for an airport in Norfolk. I'll stay there for two days. In the evening I went to Norwich. I met in the dance hall there Eileen Walker, my ex-dance partner, and I danced with her all evening. This morning I have flown for the first time since the 11th of September 1944. In the evening again to Norwich. I went to the Naafi club. It's a wonderful building.

26th of July 1945

Early in the morning, I went back to London. In the afternoon I went to Helen's place because she didn't feel good. I slept there.

27th of July 1945 in the evening I stayed at home.

28th of July 1945

Helen came to eat with us in the afternoon. Mama and Fre went to Hastings. I've cooked. It was delicious. We didn't go out because Helen didn't feel well, and I had a headache too.

30th of July 1945

In the evening I went dancing in the 'Hammerschitt Palais de Dance' for an hour. I met there a very good dancer, Kathryn.

31st of July 1945

In the evening, I've been training at Millwall. Afterwards, I went home. Helen came too. We had a delicious meal.

1st of August 1945

In the afternoon I played football. We played 3-3. I made two goals. I'm very tired. In 5he evening to the 'Brixton Empress'.

2nd of August 1945

In the afternoon I was in the park with Helen. In the evening for an hour to the Stage Door Canteen and after that at 10.30 I picked up mama from the train, she has been six days in Hastings.

3rd of August 1945

In the evening a lot of people came to visit us.

4th of August 1945

In the evening I went to Helen's place. I had to fix her bicycle and paint my own bike. Then I went to my house, and Helen stayed and slept here.

5th of August 1945

This morning we made a trip with my bike. We went to Windsor. It was a long trip but very nice. I had a breakdown, but fortunately, I found a bicycle repairman. We came back home at 9.30 and were very tired.

6th of August 1945

Bank Holiday Monday. Today I have a day off. Fre went to Hastings yesterday because she now has a week's vacation.

10th of August 1945

Today there was a rumour that the war in Japan is over too. People were crazy, but it wasn't true. Helen came to us and stayed overnight.

11th of August 1945

The whole afternoon and evening I went out with Helen.

12th of August 1945, Sunday

In the afternoon I went with Helen to the Netherlands House. In the evening we went to Maccabi. I slept at Helen's place.

13th of August 1945

Today it's an important day. This morning at 8.00 o'clock Helen and I are engaged.

15th of August 1945

TODAY THE WAR IS OVER. SO TOMORROW AND THE DAY AFTER TOMORROW IT IS V.J.DAY

16th of August 1945

V.J. DAY. The whole day I've been out with Helen. In the evening, the six of us went to Maccabi. After that to a party.

THIS IS THE END OF MY DIARY

10th of May 1940   -   15th of August 1945

Ruby - Scott - Joe - Janine - Beverley - Alex - Geoff - Ellie - Darren - Fay - Harvey - Hilary - Stuart - Gemma - Nina - Richard